Enhancing Organizational Effectiveness Through Knowledge Management and Transformational Leadership

Battogtokh Dorjgotov

Enhancing Organizational Effectiveness Through Knowledge Management and Transformational Leadership

palgrave
macmillan

Battogtokh Dorjgotov
Mongolian Academy of Sciences
Ulaanbaatar, Mongolia

ISBN 978-981-97-8038-9   ISBN 978-981-97-8039-6 (eBook)
https://doi.org/10.1007/978-981-97-8039-6

This Palgrave Macmillan imprint is published by the registered company Springer Nature Singapore Pte Ltd.
The registered company address is: 152 Beach Road, #21-01/04 Gateway East, Singapore 189721, Singapore

Contents

List of Figures

List of Tables

CHAPTER 1

Foundation of the Exploration

Abstract This chapter introduces the study, emphasizing the significance of enhancing organizational effectiveness within Research and Development (R&D) organizations. It addresses methods to improve efficiency tailored to the unique characteristics of R&D entities. The chapter provides an overview of the Mongolian Academy of Sciences (MAS), detailing its structure, human resources and legal foundations, which constitute the main subject of the research. It discusses the roles of knowledge management and transformational leadership in improving organizational effectiveness. Additionally, the chapter outlines the goals and objectives of the research, presents the conceptual framework and survey instruments and explains the importance of the proposed model along with the anticipated outcomes.

Keywords Knowledge management · Transformational leadership · Organizational effectiveness · Mediator · Moderator · Organizational culture · Organizational strategy · Technology · Human resource development

B. Dorjgotov, *Enhancing Organizational Effectiveness Through Knowledge Management and Transformational Leadership*,
https://doi.org/10.1007/978-981-97-8039-6_1

Organizations are commonly defined as instrument of purpose. Every organization has work to do and some way of measuring and communicating how well it does this work. Using the classical definition of organization every organization is set up for a particular function that is clarified through its goals (Etzioni, 1964). The goals are made visible through the results of the organization's work and activities in pursuit of these goals (Lusthaus et al., 2002). Based on goal approach, organizational effectiveness seems as the extent to which an organization is able to fulfill its goals. However, describing and measuring effectiveness presents problems in a Research and Development (R&D) organization. There are very few findings among R&D organizations on what the term "effectiveness" really means to them, how to be effective, and how it should be measured in R&D organization. The productivity of an industrial operation usually includes the quantity and quality output. However, in an R&D organization, many units of output are intangible and subjective in nature. Productivity also needs to be related to the goals of the organization. Organization effectiveness has a one-to-one correspondence to the general concept of productivity, but it also includes items which are not always included in productivity—for instance, quality and utility (Jain & Triandis, 1997). Organization should not be productive only, and it needs to be viable over a considerable period of time. This in turn requires that members be satisfied with organization. R&D organization output measures can be subjective or objective, discrete or scalar, and quantitative or non-quantitative, and there can also be qualitative aspects associated with them. The relationship of output measures to organizational goals must also be included (Jain & Triandis, 1997). Basically, an R&D organization is any group or team of professionals that develop R&D activities autonomously or inside some company or institution, and the key elements of processes that apply and develop knowledge are speed and flexibility in a rapidly changing environment (Guillermo, 2003). While a key to understanding the success and failure of organizational effectiveness within any organization is the identification and assessment of preconditions that are necessary for the effort to flourish, there are many precondition could be effect on organizational effectiveness. However, this research mainly focusing mediating effect of knowledge management and moderating effect of transformational leadership due to significant of the study. Gold et al. (2001) emphasized that the hallmark of the new economy is the ability of organizations to realize economic value from their collection of knowledge assets as well as their assets of information, production, distribution and affiliation. The knowledge management effects in an organization have become a critical factor in organization's success and competitiveness. Moreover, knowledge management has become a fundamental source of wealth creation, supplementing industrial capital and land (World Bank, 1998). It is true because we already pass the first decide of the twenty-first century, during the first decide of twenty-first-century contemporary management thinking is being profoundly reshaped by two new convictions: first, managing organizational knowledge effectively is essential to achieving competitive success; second, managing knowledge is now a central concern and must become a basic skill of the modern manager (Sanchez, 2001).

In addition, an effective leader has to generate trust and have sense a purpose in success organization. They have to face the challenges of globalization and new technology and knowledge. Basically, the leadership is a process of influencing individuals and guiding other toward desired goals (Kermally, 2002) and those leaders who have confidence in their ability to develop and stimulate followers to higher level of performance will treat them with confidence and self-esteem. Such leaders exert a positive influence and obtain better result. Elkin and Keller (2003) suggested that transformational leadership appears to be an effective leadership style for use in R&D settings. Similarly, many studies have been completed in business, industry, government, the military, educational institutions and nonprofit organizations, most of them reveals that transformational leaders were more effective and satisfying as leaders than others styles of leadership especially in R&D settings. Based on above and other concept, the study aimed to exploring among organizational culture, strategy, technology, human resource development (HRD), transformational leadership, knowledge management and organizational effectiveness using a hypothesis model. The model suggests that organizational culture, technology, organizational strategy and HRD are preconditions required for effective knowledge management. It contends that effective knowledge management, when moderated by transformational leadership, aims to further improve organizational effectiveness in R&D organizations.

1.1 Background

In 1990, during the initial stages of transition to market, main concern was to sustain a macro-economic stability, whereas today, the top priority is to develop a basis for long-term economic growth in Mongolia. In the age of knowledge-based economy, knowledge distribution power is the key to a nation's economic growth and international competitiveness. The economic theory emphasizes the accumulation of R&D and human capital in explaining economic growth (Aghion & Howitt, 1992). From this point, governments are responsible for developing the technological structure and the appropriate institutions and macro-economic policies to support R&D. In today's rapidly developing world, processing information swiftly, identifying the critical mass and investing in intellectual properties have become crucial factors of effective organizations and economic development in Mongolia (Science and Technology plan of Mongolia, 2007). Before 1990, the structure of science and technology in Mongolia closely resembled to the Soviet model (Russian model). Its three major components consisted of higher education institutions (universities and colleges), research institutes of Mongolian Academy of Sciences (MAS) and R&D institutes under branch ministries. Due to the extensive assistance provided by the former USSR until 1989, Mongolia had been able to build up a relatively large science and technology structure, including over 90 research institutions but now, there are 45 research institutes. According to the type, they were divided in the following four groups: (1) Research Institutes of MAS, (2) University Research Laboratories, (3) Public Research Institutes, and (4) Private Research Institutes. The research institutes of MAS were asked to participate in this study. The MAS is an autonomous agency under the patronage of the government and has 50 members (academicians). Recently, there are 21 research institutes of nature and as well as social sciences operated by MAS. Also MAS created two specialized Academies, the Mongolian Academy of Medical Sciences and the Mongolian Academy of Agricultural Sciences within its operational framework. About 25% of total 3562 researchers in Mongolia are working in MAS research institutes and 35.6% of total scientific expenditure is allocated to the MAS research institutes (NSTF, 2002). Figure 1.1 shows the total academic papers involvement of Mongolian R&D organizations which is concern number of cooperated and autonomic published papers between 1999 and 2009 in Mongolia.

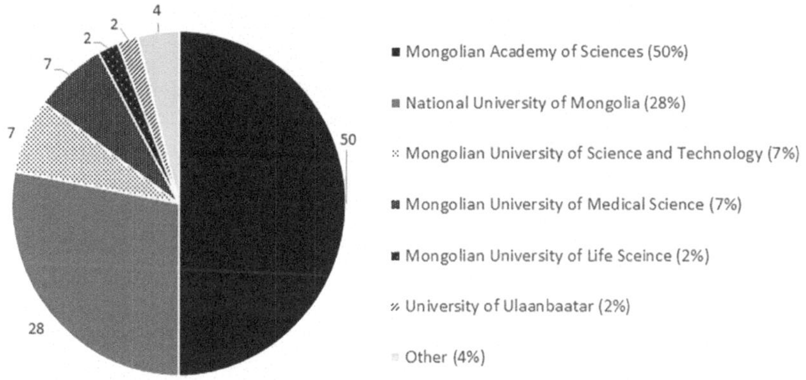

Fig. 1.1 The total academic papers involvement of Mongolian R&D organizations during 1999–2009 (Ganzorig, 2009)

Generally, according to the law "on the Legal Status of the Mongolian Academy of Sciences" passed by the Parliament (State Great Hural) of Mongolia promulgated, MAS shall responsible for the to regulate the activities of its subunits and laboratories and organize the effective fulfillment of research work ordered by the state and evaluate on a scientific basis the economic, social and political interrelationship development of the state and develop basic concepts for further directions and methods, etc. Therefore, MAS is the central institution for the development of science and advanced technology in this country as well as the central scientific think-tank whose aim is to develop science and advanced technology in the country. The Mongolian Academy of Sciences is a civil self-governed non-commercial organization.

Furthermore, understanding and measuring the impact of organization effectiveness, knowledge management, transformational leadership and organizational factors are crucial in setting of R&D management in research institutes as well as in setting of National Science & Technology policy in Mongolia. Typically, organizational effectiveness is a powerful and problematic concept. It is powerful in the sense that it represents a useful tool for critically evaluating and enhancing the work of organizations; it is problematic in the sense that it can mean different things to different people (Forbes, 1998). Especially, improving or assessing the effectiveness of R&D organizations is not easy task. For instance, the productivity of an industrial operation usually includes the quantity of its output and its quality. However, in an R&D organization, many units of outputs are intangible and subjective in nature and the multifaceted output of R&D in a nation includes indicators such as patenting rates, number of research scientists and engineers, as well as scientific publications. Knowledge management in an organization has become a critical factor in an organization's success and competitiveness. Thus, knowledge management goes beyond information management to include many other skills, competencies, cultural issues and learning. The increased innovation, creativity, collaboration, and team work have influenced the job market and created the need for an interdisciplinary approach to knowledge management education (Al-Hawamdeh, 2003). Based on organization view, leadership basically the process through which leaders influence the attitudes, behaviors and values of others toward organizational goals (Vecchio, 1995). Indeed, no one can deny its critical importance to the success of any organization. Research work on leadership in the both general leadership and in R&D management literature emphasized the importance of transformational leadership. According to Bass theory (Bass, 1985; Bass & Avolio, 1990a), transformational leaders motivate their followers to perform beyond expectation by raising the follower's confidence levels and providing support for developing to higher levels. The effective leadership's one of the key attribute is managing knowledge that leads to the creating and sharing knowledge within the organization, and this kind of leadership style might be transformational leadership and many scholars indicate that transformational leadership plays a significant role in enhancing several aspects of performance in R&D context. On the basis of above and other considerations, this study examines the joint impact of organizational factors, transformational leadership and knowledge management on organizational effectiveness in an R&D organization in Mongolia.

1.2 Purpose of the Study

The purpose of the study is to examine the impacts among organizational culture, strategy, technology, human resource development (HRD) and transformational leadership, knowledge management, organizational effectiveness by utilizing a hypotheses model in an R&D organization. The model contends that organizational culture, technology, organizational strategy, and HRD are preconditions required for effective knowledge management is mediated and that effective knowledge management

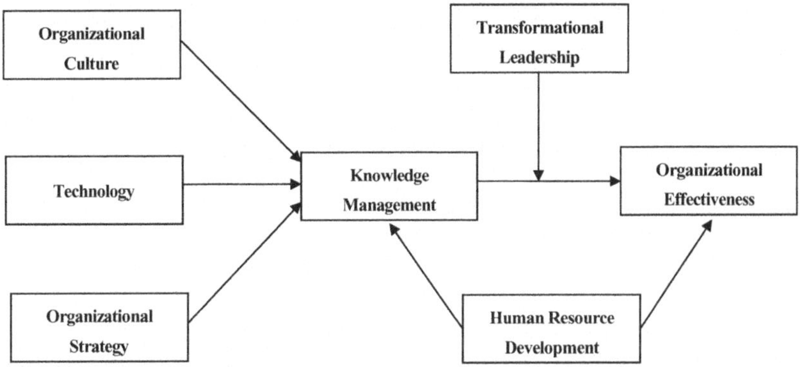

Fig. 1.2 Conceptual framework

when moderating by transformational leadership is aimed at further improvement of organizational effectiveness. The proposed relationship of the variables of interest is illustrated in Fig. 1.2.

1.3 Research Questions

The study is to find out the answers to the following main research questions:

1. What are the contributions of organizational culture, organizational strategy, technology and human resource development on organizational effectiveness?
2. What is the impact of organizational culture, organizational strategy, technology and human resource development on knowledge management?
3. What is the impact of knowledge management on organizational effectiveness?
4. How does knowledge management affect in the relationship between organizational culture, organizational strategy, technology, HRD and organizational effectiveness?
5. What is the impact of transformational leadership on organizational effectiveness?
6. How does transformational leadership affect both on knowledge management and on organizational effectiveness?

7. How do effectively manage R&D-based organization and lead to motivate researcher, scientist and engineer for successful future?

1.4 Significance of the Study

The study has both theoretical and practical significance. It adds new knowledge to management science on several fronts relating to R&D.

Theoretically, this study aims to (1) build a bridge among the literature on organizational effectiveness, knowledge management, transformational leadership, and organizational factors (such as culture, strategy, technology, and HRD); (2) provide an in-depth examination of the relationships among knowledge management, transformational leadership, and organizational effectiveness in an R&D organization; and (3) present a hypothesized model that not only illustrates the effects of knowledge management, transformational leadership, and other organizational factors on organizational effectiveness, but also suggests meaningful ways to measure organizational effectiveness in an R&D context

Practically, this study is the first formal study of evaluating organizational effectiveness in a major R&D organization of Mongolia. The results of the proposed study will assist R&D managers by pointing out areas of strengths and by highlighting the perception of effective knowledge management and transformational leadership.

Finally, the study will help R&D managers, especially who are working in Mongolian Academy of Sciences to understand major concepts of organizational theory such as effectiveness, culture, strategy, technology and HRD.

1.5 Summary

This chapter provides an introduction to the study that serves as a preface to the background, purpose of the study, significance of the study and research questions. In addition, this chapter includes explanations of the limitations of the proposed study. The literature review in Chapter 2 examines related literature and previous research findings from other studies on organizational effectiveness, knowledge management, transformational leadership and organizational factors (culture, strategy, technology and HRD). Chapter 3 discusses the methodology of the study and includes description of the research design, instrument, operational definitions, variables' measurement, data collection procedure and data analysis procedures. The research hypotheses and constitutive definitions have also been provided to further explain to intend of the study. Results of the data collection and subsequent analysis are reported in Chapter 4, and a discussion and conclusion of those results are presented in Chapter 5.

CHAPTER 2

Insights from the Field

Abstract This chapter provides a comprehensive review of previous studies and literature related to the research questions and hypotheses. It is organized into eight sections, focusing on key components: R&D, organizational effectiveness, knowledge management, transformational leadership, organizational culture, organizational strategy, technology and HRD. The literature review begins with an exploration of R&D theories and the role of R&D organizations in advancing knowledge and innovation. It then examines three organizational outcomes: organizational effectiveness, effective knowledge management and effective transformational leadership. The review also delves into four key organizational factors (organizational culture, strategy, technology and HRD) discussing their definitions, impacts and interrelationships. Finally, the chapter explicates how these variables interact to influence organizational performance, providing a solid theoretical foundation for the study.

Keywords Knowledge management · Transformational leadership · Organizational effectiveness · Mediator · Moderator · Organizational culture · Organizational strategy · Technology · Human resource development

B. Dorjgotov, *Enhancing Organizational Effectiveness Through Knowledge Management and Transformational Leadership*, https://doi.org/10.1007/978-981-97-8039-6_2

The purpose of this chapter is to present a review of previous studies and literature related to research questions and hypotheses. The chapter is divided into eight components that focus on the R&D, organizational effectiveness, knowledge management, transformational leadership organizational culture, organizational strategy, technology and human resource development. The literature review is organized around the concept and their interrelationships as follows: firstly, the R&D setting which means relating research & development organization theories and literatures; secondly, three organizational outcomes of organizational effectiveness, effective knowledge management and effective transformational leadership; thirdly, the four organizational factors—organizational culture, organizational strategy, technology and human resource development; and finally, the literature review explicates the interrelations among variables.

2.1 Research and Development

Research and development (R&D) covers many different activities of basic research, applied R&D. The OCED defines R&D as creative work undertaken in a systematic basis in order to increase the stock of knowledge of man, culture and society, and the use of this stock of knowledge to dive into new applications. In order to provide functional and understandable definitions for various research activities, science indicators categorized R&D activities as efforts in science and engineering as follows: producing significant advances across the broad front of understanding of natural and social phenomena its basic research, fostering inventive activity to produce technological advances its applied R&D and combining understanding and invention in the form of socially useful and affordable products and processes its innovation (OECD, 1993).

Moreover, Drongelen et al. (1996) defined that R&D, in its broadest sense, is the process of transforming customer demands and technological advancements (inputs) into new product designs (outputs). Economic theory demonstrates the accumulation of R&D and human capital in explaining economic growth (Aghon & Howitt, 1992). Griffith et al. (2000) empirical research showing that the rate of return on R&D affects productivity through innovation. Their study also highlights the practical importance for firms of both innovation and technology transfer as two potential sources of productivity growth in different countries. Moreover,

Griffith et al. (2000) provide econometric evidence that R&D expenditure plays a role in assimilating the research discoveries of others as well as its conventional role as a source of innovation. Currently, empirical literature observed (Godin & Doré, 2006), the public R&D has a wide spectrum of socio-economic impacts, for instance, scientific impacts, technological impacts, economic impacts, cultural impacts, societal impacts, policy impacts, organizational impacts, health impacts, environmental impacts, symbolic impacts and training impacts.

In addition, a R&D organization is any group or team of professionals that develop R&D activities autonomously or inside some company or institution (Guillermo, 2003). According to Jain and Triandis (1997), four basic elements are required for an R&D organization namely people, ideas, funds and cultural elements. These four basic ingredients have to be coordinated with skill by the management of R&D organizations in order to achieve high productivity and excellence. It is obvious that the most important element is creative people. Such people have the bright ideas and skills to do research and then translate research results into useful products. In this case, in an organization may need some kind of effective knowledge management to the people to improving their bright ideas and skills. However, these people must be organized into structured that permit effective cooperation. In doing so it is important to keep in mind that certain mixes of people work better than others and it may request some kind of effective leadership to the organization. To ensure a smoothly functioning organization, one needs unstated assumptions, beliefs, norms and values—in other words, an organizational culture that will favor creativity and innovation. Last, but not least, one needs funds. The R&D activity can be carried out under various financing systems and funds, for example, signing contracts with external customers, internally with the objective of developing infrastructure or new products for the company, financed by the government within national development plans, or as research professors in higher educational institutions or universities.

2.2 Organizational Effectiveness

Cameron (1980) stated that evaluating the effectiveness of organizations requires selecting the appropriate criteria. Many approaches are available, but to find the most useful approach, the evaluator should first answer. He has emphasized that an organizational effectiveness can rarely improve until it is clear what effectiveness is and what criteria have been used to define it. Maybe one firm's effectiveness is another firm's failure. Moreover, according to Forbes (1998), organizational effectiveness is powerful yet problematic concept. It is powerful in the sense that it represents a useful tool for critically evaluating and enhancing the work of organizations; it is problematic in the sense that it can means different things to different people. Some previous research provides consensus about how to make functionalize the concept of organizational effectiveness. For instance, Scott (1977) and Campbell (1987) defined the organizational effectiveness is a multifarious construct and the fact that organizations are very complex settings explains why there are such a variety of perspectives with which to approach the definition and measurements of effectiveness. However, there has been no agreement about the best approach to define and measure effectiveness (Bedeian & Zammuto, 1991; Marlene, 2002), and generally, the evaluators have used four major approaches namely goal, system resource, internal process & operation, and strategic constituencies (multiple constituencies) to define and assess organizational effectiveness (Cameron, 1980; Cameron & David, 1983). Importantly, the several authors have maintained that effectiveness does not exist apart from the context of the organization. Therefore, it should be defined and measured contextually not universally, even if doing so limits comparisons between studies (Backer & Gerhart, 1996; Ferris et al., 1998; Roger & Wright, 1998).

Scholars emphasized that the most widely used approach defines effectiveness in terms of how well an organization accomplished its goals (Cameron, 1980; Lusthaus et al., 2002; Zammuto, 1982). Goals are the central component of this approach. Thus, operative goals are clearly identifiable, consensual, assessable and time-bounded and are the most important features to focus on when evaluating organizational effectiveness (Price, 1972; Zammuto, 1982). Especially, improving or assessing the effectiveness of R&D and governmental organizations is no easy task. Given that we define effectiveness as the extent to which an organization is meeting its functional goals. As stated by Lusthaus et al. (2002), at one level the organizational goals are self-evident, for instance: universities provide high learning in a country. However, describing and measuring effectiveness presents problems: first, it is unclear whether you can decide on a single set goal or, for that matter, come to consensus about multiple set goals for an organization (Brown, 1994), and second, it is unclear where to go, and to whom to go to, to identify goals or seek consensus. Despite these difficulties, organizations do engage in a variety processes to identify goals, objectives and systems to communicate their effectiveness—that is the extent to which they attain their goals—to their constituents (Lusthaus et al., 2002). So, when we assess the effectiveness of an organization, it is important to first understand its functional purpose and then explore the way the organization understands the various dimensions. Trying to appreciate the dimensions of organizational effectiveness requires some understanding of functional purposes of the category of organizations within which the organization fits, these functional purposes give insight into the dimensions of organizational effectiveness (Lusthaus et al., 2002) and the quest then becomes to develop organizational effectiveness indices which are reflective of sector with such diversity and challenge. Moreover, Steers (1975) suggested a clear understanding of an organization's functional and environmental uniqueness is a prerequisite to assessing its effectiveness.

Gold and his colleagues (2001) attempt to functionalize new concept for organizational effectiveness. They (Gold et al., 2001) demonstrated that organizational effectiveness includes activities such as improved ability to innovate, improved coordination of efforts, and rapid commercialization of new product, and that external factors (e.g., overall economic growth, industry growth and profitability, level and intensity of competition, consumer preferences) as well as factors internal to the firm (e.g., cost structure, revenue, firm size, efficiency) can contribute to overall effectiveness (Smith, 2006). Gold et al. (2001) concluded that three important processes of organizational effectiveness are efficiently, adaptability and innovativeness. Economists define efficiency as the absence of waste and explain that an efficient economy or firm is one which "utilizes all its available resources and produces the maximum amount of output that its technology permits" (Baumol & Blinder, 1994). Adaptability is the change in a significant organizational attribute, such as basic business strategy or organizational structure in response to environmental change. The innovations are a measure of knowledge management effectiveness; reflect a degree of uniqueness; and generally give rise to a new or modified device, system, program, process, etc. for adaptation to the organization (Smith, 2006).

Regretfully, not many solutions have been proposed and tested in the R&D-based organization to evaluate the organizational effectiveness. In the early literature, Mahoney and Weitzel (1969) observed the different criteria of "general business" and "R&D" for organizational effectiveness. Their (Mahoney & Weitzel, 1969) studies show the difference between

R&D and general business models of organizational effectiveness can be understood in terms of a hierarchical complex of criterion measures on the ultimate criterion at the apex of the hierarchy. Typically, the ultimate organizational effectiveness refers to long-run goal achievement. This achievement is difficult to measure in the short run because the goal sought broad and general and thus difficult to define in terms of specific measures. In addition, Mahoney and Weitzel (1969) identified that the general business managers tend to use productivity, planning, initiation and reliable, efficient performance as close substitutes for ultimate criterion of effectiveness. On the other hand, the R&D managers tend to use cooperative behavior, staff development and reliably performance as higher-order criteria and efficiency, productivity and output behavior as lover-order criteria (Mahoney & Weitzel, 1969). Both groups' managers look to the same general midrange criteria, but they arrange these criteria in different hierarchical levels of relationship to the ultimate criterion of overall organizational effectiveness. This study suggested that R&D managers might need to share a common concept of the ultimate criterion of organizational effectiveness with general business managers and be equally concerned about long-run profitable performance of the entire organization. The findings here indicate that the global criterion of overall effectiveness is a function of a set of more specific dimensions, which vary from one setting to another. Effectiveness can refer to the successful accomplishment of an intended result. Therefore, an effective organization should be successful in accomplishing result and must be managed by a successful manager. However, except Mahoney and Weitzel (1969) study there seems to be very little agreement among R&D organization and management scientists on what the term "effectiveness" really means, what to do to achieve it, and how it should be measured in an R&D organization. To an academician or a research scientist, effectiveness may be defined in terms of number of books or papers published or inventions and new ideas discovered in the research institutes. Jain and Triandis (1997) emphasized the productivity of an industrial operation usually includes the quantity of its output and its quality. However, in an R&D organization, many units of output are intangible and subjective in nature. Productivity also needs to relate to the objectives and goals of the organization. Organization effectiveness has a one-to-one correspondence to the general concept of productivity, but it also includes items not always included in productivity—for instance, quality and utility. Using this definition, it seems if an organization is very effective, it is very productive, and if it is not very effective, then it is not very productive. Not only should an organization be productive, but it needs to be viable over a considerable period of time. This in turn requires that members be satisfied with organization (Jain & Triandis, 1997). They suggested determining criteria of organizational effectiveness in R&D laboratories (see Table 2.1). The criteria listed in Table 2.1 are self-evident. However, Jain and Triandis (1997) give some comments to concerning of the congruence of individual and organizational goals and the use of the profit as a criterion. First, consider the congruence of individual and organizational goals.

Table 2.1 Criteria of organizational effectiveness in R&D laboratories

Criterion	*Measurement instrument*
Quantity of output	Number of reports, publications, new products
Quality of the work	Number of patents obtained, number of times publications of lab members are quoted, number of refereed publications per member of lab
Increases in the size of organization	Obtained more research funds
Absenteeism	Number of persons out of the total workforce who are absent without a valid excuse on an average day (counted inversely)
Level of stress	Measured with physiological indexes, number of visits to hospital, frequency of peptic ulcers, etc. (counted inversely)
Level of job satisfaction	Measured with a standardized questionnaire, such as the Job Descriptive Index. Components: Satisfaction with pay, supervisor, organization or company, job, co-workers, working conditions
Pride in the organization	Feelings of pride measured via questionnaires
Congruence of individual and organizational goals	The extent individual goals are consistent with goals as they are reflected in employee and management statements
Profit	Direct profit or return on investment studies where returns are determined from implementation of research products

If the individual's activities are quite consistent with the activities and goals of the organization, this will result in a better organization than one in which individuals try to do their own thing and are not really concerned with what happens to the organization. Next consider profit, for a profit-oriented organization, revenues or earnings may provide a good measure of its productivity or effectiveness. R&D organization output measures can be subjective or objective, discrete or scalar, and quantitative or non-quantitative, and there can also be qualitative aspects associated with them. Additionally, the relationship between output measures and organizational goals should be considered. However, purpose of this review is not to provide a new conceptualization of effectiveness or argue for superior methods of measurement. Instead, it aims to argue for appropriate conceptualization and measurement for a particular context of organizational effectiveness in the selected objective area. Thus, this study utilized the dimensions of efficiency, adaptability and innovations which are very suitable for the R&D organizational effectiveness.

2.3 Knowledge Management

In the field of knowledge management (KM), multiple different attempts to categorize, classify and define knowledge, and related terms have been undertaken in the past and are still questioned. When the literature focused on knowledge management, the discussions often concern the characteristics of knowledge, the difference between information of knowledge and categorization of knowledge. Some authors define knowledge as 'justified true belief' (Irma & Rajiv, 2001), while a common expression for knowledge is 'information in action' (Kucza, 2001), referring to information applied for a specific purpose. Nonaka (1994) and Huber (1991) defined knowledge as a justified personal belief that enhances an individual's capacity to take effective action, which may be a more appropriate definition and can be applied across various fields. The knowledge has various shapes, according to Nonaka and Takeuchi (1995), there is a difference between tacit and explicit knowledge. Tacit knowledge is knowledge in the human mind and it is difficult to externalize or mediate. Explicit knowledge is formalized knowledge, i.e., knowledge recorded as video, in a document, etc. and usually covers part of the original tacit knowledge but is not a full representation of it. In addition, Kucza (2001) emphasized that tacit knowledge can be transferred throughout any direct face-to-face communication between people or by transmuting it into explicit knowledge and sharing according to artifact. The transformation back to tacit knowledge takes place during the reading and understanding of explicit knowledge. Following the implications of the process-oriented perspective, knowledge is seen as a dynamic factor by social interaction between individuals and organizations. Knowledge is active because it is action oriented and subjective because knowledge is information in a certain context.

Irma and Rajiv (2001) defined the effective knowledge management (KM) is considered key to the success of contemporary organizations. Similarly, Sanchez (2001) emphasized that first decide of the twenty-first century, contemporary management thinking is being profoundly reshaped by two new convictions: First, managing organizational knowledge effectively is essential to achieving competitive success; second, managing knowledge is now a central concern and must become a basic skill of the modern manager. Importantly, organizations may not be equally predisposed for successful launch and maintenance of knowledge management initiatives. Therefore, a key to understanding the success and failure of knowledge management within organization is the identification and assessment of preconditions that are necessary for the effort to flourish. These preconditions are described broadly as capabilities or resources within the organizational behavior literatures (Gold et al., 2001; Nonaka, 1991, 1994). Carrillo et al. (2004) emphasized that knowledge management is the continuous process of managing all knowledge in order to anticipate current and future needs, to identify and exploit existing and acquired knowledge as well as develop new opportunities. Similarly, Rastogi (2000) defined knowledge management as "systematic and integrative process of coordinating organization-wide activities of acquiring, creating, storing, sharing, diffusing, developing and deploying knowledge by individuals and groups in pursuit of major organizational goals". Moreover, Alavi and Leidner (2001) defined that the knowledge management refers to a systemic and organizationally specified process for acquiring, organizing and communicating both tacit and explicit knowledge of employees so that other employees may make use of it to be more effective and productive in their work. Accordingly, there are many possible approaches to research on KM. However, most of the scholars use process-oriented approach as we see in literature review. Therefore, the approach selected for this research was to look at the processes taking place within KM with the goal of developing a representation that is simultaneously both simple and comprehensive enough. Gold and his colleagues (Gold et al., 2001) developed many characteristic features of knowledge process capabilities. These features include creative application of technology; knowledge integration and coordination; ability to create and apply knowledge; ability to acquire knowledge; ability to organize knowledge; ability to generate knowledge; ability to combine resources and capabilities; and ability to convert, retain and protect knowledge. Based on their evaluation of characteristics, Gold et al. (2001) suggested that acquisition, conversion, application and protection are the main conditions of knowledge process capabilities. According to the above different characteristics of KM, the appropriate definition might be knowledge management as the overall task of managing the process of knowledge creation (acquisition), conversion, utilization and protection, as well as the related activities. Knowledge creation process (also called acquisition, generation): Many terms have been used to describe these processes: acquire, seek, generate, acquisition, capture and collaborate. All of these terms have a common theme the accumulation of knowledge (Gold et al., 2001). The first consideration is to create (acquire) knowledge, to aim at managing and controlling the interest of stakeholders (customers, supplier, public institution and competitors) and to influence the participation of these stakeholders in the knowledge management process (Lee & Suh, 2003). Moreover, Alavi and Leidner (2001), observed organizational knowledge creation, involve developing new content or replacing existing content within the organization's tacit and explicit knowledge. In this study, we used the definition of creation (acquisition) process refers to the organization's effort to gather information and new knowledge from internal and external sources and codify it into explicit knowledge (Lee & Sukoco, 2007). Knowledge sharing process (also called conversion): the sharing of knowledge in organizations or departments is one of the fundamental functions of any knowledge management program. The knowledge sharing (conversion) process refers to a set of actions related to the transformation of knowledge from one to another and consists of two types of knowledge such as tacit knowledge and explicit knowledge (Lee et al., 2004). For instance, these two types of knowledge transform into different kinds of knowledge. Tacit knowledge is highly personal and hard to formalize, making it difficult to communicate or share with others (Nonaka & Konno, 1998). Therefore, tacit knowledge can usually be shared through a highly interactive conversation. In addition, new knowledge is often created throughout the combination of the shared knowledge with the receiver's existing knowledge (Nonaka & Takeuchi, 1995). The process-oriented approach focuses on the individual as the most important actor when knowledge is created. Nonaka (1991, 1994) observed a key task in making the knowledge of the individual available to the rest of the organization. He suggested focusing on the creative individual, who is perceived as the most essential actor in knowledge creation when managing knowledge within an organization. According to the Davenport and Prusak (1998) knowledge sharing is the knowledge exchange activities among organizational units (individuals, groups, organizations) for current or future benefits. In this study, we used the definition of knowledge sharing that refers to a set of actions related to the transformation of knowledge from one to another and consists of two types of knowledge such as tacit knowledge and explicit knowledge for current and future benefits. Knowledge utilization process (also called knowledge application): we know that the utilization of the knowledge rather than in the knowledge itself. Batt (2001) stated that "knowledge utilization means making knowledge more active and relevant for the firm in creating value" and that knowledge in an organization needs to be applied to organizations' products, processes and services. More commonly knowledge utilization is a process that is oriented toward actual use of the knowledge (Gold et al., 2001) which is used in this study. Knowledge Protection Process: the issues of knowledge utilization, conversion and creations have concerns for those aware of security and protection of these knowledge assets. A serious question today is whether organizations are properly planning to protect both the explicit knowledge stored in information technology, the transference pipeline, and the tacit knowledge in the minds of their employees. If these perceptions can be better understood, new strategies to help organizations plan for better protection and security of their knowledge can be explored and developed (Jeffrey, 2003). Gold et al. (2001) defined that security-oriented processes are designed to protect the knowledge from inappropriate or illegal use or from theft. Protection is vital if the knowledge is used to generate or preserve a competitive advantage. Therefore, in this study we used the definition of knowledge protection refers to protect the knowledge from inappropriate or illegal use or from theft.

2.4 Transformational Leadership

Based on organization view, leadership is basically the process through which leaders influence the attitudes, behaviors and values of others toward organizational goals (Lusthaus et al., 2002). Indeed, no one can deny its critical importance to the success of any organization. The leadership is one of the most complex concept studied by organizational and psychological researchers and is attested to by the many different definitions of leadership that one finds in the literature. Generally, some of these definitions describe leadership as an act of influence, some as a process, and yet others have looked at a person's trait qualities (Johns & Moser, 1989). Each one of these approaches to leadership attempts to describe the nature and characteristics of leadership. The leadership has been accompanied throughout time by numerous theories that have been categorized into several historically distinct approaches that focus either on traits, behavior, situational contingencies or cultural contingencies. Certainly, each theory and approach has been developed and described by different authors and have used different classifications. Since, it is not intention of this review to give detailed descriptions of the different leadership approaches or ideas, except "multifactor leadership" theory, due to research interesting of "transformational leadership" style. Multifactor leadership theory developed by Bass in the 1980s encompasses a range of leader behaviors. This approach incorporates the: transformational, transactional, laissez-faire leadership and charismatic styles of leadership. These leadership styles have been described to have a direct effect on individual and organizational level outcomes (Bass, 1990; Yukl, 2008; Yukl & Van Fleet, 1992). These leadership styles have been described to have a direct effect on individual and organizational level outcomes (Bass, 1990; Bass & Avolio, 1990a, 1990b; Burns, 1978; Yukl & Van Fleet, 1992). The concept of transformational was first articulated by Burns (1978) in a political science context and later formulated into a theory of leadership in organizations by Bass (1985). According to Burns (1978), transformational leaders as those who motivate their followers to perform beyond expectation by raising the follower's confidence levels and providing support for developing high levels. The research of Bass and his colleagues (Bass, 1985; Bass & Avolio, 1994, 1995) expanded Burns's factors of leadership, and they have identified five factors which the behavioral components of transformational leadership: idealized attributes, idealized influence, inspirational motivation, intellectual stimulation and individualized consideration. Idealized attributes (some called attributed charisma) are characteristics of mutual respect between the leader and followers. Therefore, transformational leaders demonstrate the following effects on followers: (a) instill a sense of pride in followers, (b) go beyond their own interests for the improvement of the group, (c) act in ways that build respect from others, (d) show a sense of authority and expertise while making personal sacrifices for the common cause and (e) encourage and build confidence to the followers. Idealized influence refers to leaders behave in ways that result in their being role models for their followers. The leaders are admired, respected and trusted. Followers identify with the leaders and want to emulate them. Inspirational motivation refers to leaders behave in ways that motivate and inspire those around them by providing meaning and challenge to their followers' work. The leader creates clearly communicated expectations that followers want to meet and also demonstrates commitment to goals and the shared vision. Intellectual stimulation refers to leaders stimulate their followers' efforts to be innovative and creative by questioning assumptions, reframing problems and approaching old situations in new ways and creativity is encouraged. Followers are encouraged to try new approaches, and their ideas are not criticized because they differ from leaders' ideas. Individualized consideration occurs when leaders pay special attention to each individual's needs for achievement and growth by acting as coach or mentor. Followers and colleagues are developed to successively higher levels of potential. The leader's behavior demonstrates acceptance of individual differences (e.g., some employees receive more encouragement, some more autonomy, others firmer standards, and still others more task structure). Importantly, Bass and his colleagues (1990b) identified transformational leaders who inspire followers with vision of what can be accomplished through extra personal effort, thus motivating followers to achieve more than they thought they would achieve. Also those leaders have the ability to motivate their subordinates to commit themselves to performance beyond expectations. In this study, we used the definition of transformational leadership as the process of influencing major changes in attitudes and assumptions of organizational members and building commitment for the organization's mission and objectives. Transformational leaders are said to appeal to higher ideals and moral values of followers, heighten their expectations and spur them to greater effort and performance on behalf of the organization (Bass, 1990; Bass & Avolio, 1990b; Yukl, 1989).

Elkin and Keller (2003) suggested that transformational leadership appears to be an effective leadership style for use in R&D settings. One of the key attributes of effective leadership is managing knowledge that leads to creating and sharing knowledge among organization and this type of leadership style could be defined as a transformational leadership. For instance, transformational leaders' traits of inspirational motivation and intellectual stimulation are critical for organizational innovation. Moreover, many scholars indicate that transformational leadership plays a significant role in enhancing several aspects of performance in R&D context. Recently, Berson and Lenton (2005) investigated the relationship between leadership styles (transformational and transactional) and the establishment of a quality environment in an R&D setting. Their study found that transformational leadership is better than transactional leadership for support the development of a quality environment as well as satisfaction in R&D environments. The above and others studies indicate that transformational leadership could play a significant role in enhancing several aspects of performance in an R&D organization. In addition, some researchers investigated the relationship between transformational leadership and knowledge management. Crawford and his colleagues' (Crawford, 2005; Crawford & Strohkirch, 2000; Crawford et al., 2003) series of articles found that transformational leadership was significantly related to outcome innovation. Because innovation is the ability to create and manage information and knowledge, innovation is also often assumed to be one of the important characteristics of knowledge managers. Crawford's (2005) recent research emphasized that transformational leaders are better suited to handle even the most technical aspects of the modern workplace than are transactional or laissez-faire leaders. Additionally, as individual leaders move up in an organization they are better suited to engage in knowledge management, because they are more transformational in leadership style.

2.5 Organizational Factors

This section reviews research on the four organizational factors involved in this study: organizational culture, organizational strategy, technology and human resource development (HRD). Each factor is examined in light of its impact on organizational effectiveness and knowledge management.

2.5.1 *Organizational Culture*

In previous scholars' study, multiple conceptualizations of organizational culture can be found in the literature. However, it is difficult to find the most appropriate perspective to assess culture where the interest is on relating culture to organizational effectiveness and knowledge management within the study area. Typically, researchers have agreed that culture can be thought of as a set of cognitions shared by members of a social unit (Hause, 2000). It is concept, and there is no concrete way to "prove" what a concept is organizational culture. There is no method for conclusively ending debates about "single true definition or concept of organizational culture (Ott, 1989). However, the multitude of definitions have been proposed by many authors (Denison, 1990; Keesing, 1974; Ott, 1989; Schein, 1981) by creating a typology of organizational culture, but some of them were collapsed during the past research period. Schein (1990) points out that multiple cultures are possible in an organization and he defined culture as a pattern of basic assumptions; invented, discovered or developed by a given group; as it learns to cope with its problems of external adaptation and internal integration; that has worked well enough to be considered valid and, therefore, is to be taught to new members as the correct way to perceive, think and feel in relation to those problems. However, Reichers and Schneider (1990) clarified the Schein's definition as learned responses to the group's problems of survival and internal integration. The responses are subconscious, taken for granted and shared by the members of the group. Ott (1989) stated that organizational culture can be defined functionally or pragmatically as a social force that controls patterns of organizational behavior by shaping members' cognitions and perceptions of meaning and realities, providing affective energy for mobilization, and identifying who belongs and who does not. The functional definition of organizational culture is quite straightforward. A functional definition provides important understandings about the functions organizational culture performs and why organizational cultures continue to exist. Nevertheless, it is far from adequate by itself for those who would work with and in organizational cultures (Ott, 1989). Sociologists, social anthropologists and social psychologists have often presented culture and ideology as integral features of the functioning of a society. Each of these authors focused on culture as a critical aspect of the adaptation of social organizations, and viewed culture as a system of "socially transmitted behavior patterns that serve to relate human communities to their ecological settings" (Keesing, 1974; Schein, 1990). From other points, organizational culture is a source of sustained competitive advantage and empirical research shows that it is a key factor to organizational effectiveness (Denison, 1990; Denison & Mishra, 1995; Denison et al., 2003; Zheng et al., 2009). This paper applies the culture framework developed by Denison and his colleagues (Denison, 1990; Denison & Mishra, 1995; Denison et al., 2003; Fey & Denison, 2003) which is very essential to the relationship between organizational culture and effectiveness. Denison and his colleagues (Denison, 1990; Denison & Mishra, 1995; Denison et al., 2003) identified and validated four traits of organizational cultures; involvement, consistency, adaptability and mission. The involvement dimension has as its central idea that effectiveness is a function of the level of involvement or participation of the members of the organization. Denison (1990) draws this view from Human Relations theory, which argues that high involvement is associated with a sense of ownership or responsibility. In turn, the sense of ownership/responsibility is associated with commitment to the organization and less need for overt control system. Denison characterizes a high involvement group as a "clan" and theorizes that beliefs, norms, and traditions govern transactions in a clan. A clan leads to a management system that capitalizes on emergent consensus, which minimizes transaction costs. The consistency dimension emphasized the value of a "strong" culture; a shared system of beliefs, values and symbols that are understood by the members of the organization. Consistency is thought to have a positive impact on the group's ability to reach consensus and carry out coordinated action. The fundamental concept is that implicit control systems based on internalized values are a more effective way to achieve coordination among the members than explicit control system such as rules and regulations. Consistency leads to shared meaning and thus better communication and implicit coordination and control behaviors. The adaptability dimension refers to the trial and error of the adaptive process that leads to changes in culture. The absence of the ability to adapt to the culture leads to rigid bureaucracy. There are three necessary aspects to adaptability, all of which are supported by the culture, all of which have an impact on organizational effectiveness: first, the ability to perceive and respond to the external environment (e.g., customers); second, adaptability requires the ability to respond to internal customers; third, both the previous abilities require the ability to restructure and institutionalize behavior to successfully adapt. The final way of looking at the relationships between culture and effectiveness provided by Denison (1990) is the mission dimension. The mission is the shared definition of the function and purpose of the organization and its members. Mission has two major influences on organizational functioning: first, it provides purpose and meaning, and secondly it provides direction and goals. Typically, two of the dimensions, namely involvement and adaptability, are indicators of flexibility, openness and responsiveness, and were strong predictors of growth. The other two hypotheses (traits), consistency and mission, are indicators of integration, direction and vision, and were better predictors of profitability. Each of the four traits (dimensions) were also significant predictors of other effectiveness criteria such as quality, employee satisfaction and overall performance (Denison & Mishra, 1995).

Many studies raise the issue of organizational culture's influence on knowledge management success. Although, a few investigate the way in which this influence manifests itself which means the relationship between organizational culture and knowledge management. Gold's (2001) research review of the cultural environment conductive to knowledge management, suggested that shaping culture is central in a firm's ability to manage its knowledge more effectively. At any organization the interaction between individuals is essential in the innovation process. For example, dialogues between individuals or groups are often the basis for the creation of new ideas; therefore, it can be viewed as potential for creating knowledge. Turban and Aronson (2001) emphasize that "the ability of an organization to learn, develop memory, and share knowledge is dependent on its culture". Nonaka and his colleagues (Nonaka, 1994; Nonaka & Konno, 1998; Nonoka & Takeuchi, 1995) identified the type of employee interaction and collaboration is important when attempting to transmit tacit knowledge between individuals or convert tacit knowledge into explicit knowledge, thereby transforming it from individuals to organizational level. Alavi et al. (2005) investigated to explore how organizational culture influences knowledge management practices based on empirical study. The study importantly suggests that cultural values seem to influence a firm's approaches to knowledge management (Alavi et al., 2005). There have been very few studies examining the relationship between the four cultural dimensions (as identified by Denison and his colleagues) and knowledge management. Zheng et al. (2009) used Denison' cultural dimensions on his research and empirical study resulted there has a strongest positive and significant relationship between organizational culture and knowledge management. In this study, we used Denison's four dimensions of organizational culture model that depicts culture in terms of involvement, consistence, adaptability and mission.

2.5.2 *Organizational Strategy*

Strategies are often developed at different levels with different perspectives. In the early literature, the strategy refers to the determination of the basic long-term goals and objectives of the enterprise and the adoption of action and the allocation of resources necessary for carrying out these goals". Most of the scholars (Miles & Snow, 1978; Snow & Hambrick, 1980) suggested that researchers should view strategy as a pattern in the organization's important decisions and actions. Typically, these decisions will be directed at (1) maintaining the organization's alignment with its environment and (2) managing its major internal interdependencies. Defining strategy in this manner allows researchers to move beyond the abstract and normative aspects of strategy toward those decisions which actually involve organizational goals and the allocation of resources necessary to achieve goals (Snow & Hambrick, 1980). In order that, the strategy is understood as the pattern or plan that integrates an organization's major goals, policies and action sequence into a cohesive whole, it is the high level long-term meta-plan by which the ultimate success and viability of an organization (Quinn, 1980). The organizational strategy perspective investigated on different views of study such as evolution strategy, competitive advantage strategy, corporate strategy, resource-based strategy, business strategy and knowledge creation strategy so on. The evolution perspective view on strategy developed by Berney et al. (1994) is not inherently in contradiction with most theories of strategic management and most rationales favored by a particular theory-efficiency, power, market position, distinctive capabilities or whatever-usually can be understood in evolutionary perspective. Another view of strategy perspective is competitive advantage, this strategic view developed by Porter (1985) and Yamin et al. (1997). Porter (1985) proposed generic strategies by which a firm can develop a competitive advantage and create a defensible position. These strategies are (1) cost leadership, (2) differentiation and (3) focus. Porter argued that by adeptly pursuing the cost leadership, differentiation or focus strategies, businesses can attain significant and enduring competitive advantage over their rivals (Dess et al.,

1984; Porter, 1985; Speed, 1989; Yamin et al., 1997). Andrews (1998) noted that corporate strategy is the pattern of decisions within a company that determines and reveals its objectives, purposes, or goals; establishes the primary policies and plans for achieving those goals; and defines the range of businesses the company aims to pursue. It also outlines the type of economic and humanorganization the company is or aspires to be, and the nature of both economic and noneconomic contributions it intends to make to its shareholders, employees, customers, and communities. Moreover, Andrews (1971) and later Berney (1991) developed recourse based view strategy. The basis of the resource-based perspective is well established and draws from concepts in both the economic and strategy literature. The resource-based perspective also draws from the notion of Strengths, Weaknesses, Opportunities and Threats (SWOT) analysis developed by early strategists in which strategy formulation progresses by analyzing the "fit" between a firm's positioning of its internal strengthen and weaknesses with the environment's external opportunities and threats (Andrews, 1971; Ansoff, 1965). Barney (1991) explicit notion provided to describe that firm resources include a broad array of assets, capabilities, organizational processes, firm attributes and other characteristics that improve organizational effectiveness and efficiency. These attributes were classified into three categories encompassing physical capital (e.g., technology), human capital (e.g., training, experience, intelligence and judgment of individual managers) and organizational capital (e.g., formal reporting structure, informal relations among group). Barney (1991) future argued that firm resources will lead to sustained competitive advantage when they are valuable, rare, without substitutes and bundled in a manner such that the firm's resources, and thus strategies, are inimitable by current and future competitors. In the recent literatures, Short et al. (2003) emphasized that resource-based perspective assumes that firms' performance is a function of holding and deploying unique resources. Based on the desire to equip firms with scarce resources that will lead to superior performance, managerial choices drive the resource accumulation process. This view is well documented in the strategic management literature, and it draws from classic economic thought as well. Moreover, they propose that characteristics of strategic group membership moderate the relationship between firm resources and performance. That is, the ability of resources to enhance firm performance is dependent on the core on the characteristics of a strategic group. For example, in the pharmaceutical industry, a capability in R&D is necessary if the firm shares membership in a group where high R&D spending is a core characteristic that defines the group. However, for the firm to achieve differentiation on innovation, it will have to spend more on R&D than other group members (Short et al., 2003). Moreover, knowledge-based resource is one of the key resources that are central to competitive advantage (Barney, 1991). Mainly strategies could be developed at the corporate, business and functional levels. This business strategy would aim at obtaining superior financial performance and would attempt to have a sustainable advantage over competitors, and functional strategies (Hax & Majluf, 1996). At the functional level, presumably, goals, objectives and specific actions will be formulated.

In research organization or in academia, perspectives similar to corporation are relevant. A research unit would correspond to functional level, and it would need to understand and respond to requirements postulated at high level that are consistent with overall research institutes, university and college education missions. Therefore, this literature reviews more insight to investigating what kind organizational strategy is more comfortable with research area. Finally, Yang and his colleagues (2009) recently developed organizational knowledge creation strategy using EICE model, this model includes the dimensions of exploration, institutional entrepreneurship, combination and exploitation. So, this model based on knowledge creation theory (knowledge-based view). Their main contributions to organization theory were extending Nonaka's knowledge creation theory to form a new strategic model for knowledge creation. While static knowledge-based resource is important in explaining how existing knowledge can be exploited and replicated to affect certain organizational outcome, the dynamic perspective on knowledge that emphasizing how new knowledge leads to generation of novel organizational outcomes is also evoked by knowledge management researchers (Nonaka & Takeuchi, 1995).

If knowledge can be seen as a creation process that is an important determinant of organizational performance, then knowledge creation strategies are likely to be a key area of strategic choice for the organization. Moreover, many executives and managers are stressed to articulate the relationship between their firm's competitive strategy and its intellectual resources and capabilities. They do not have well-developed strategic models that help them to link knowledge creation processes to business strategy, and they are not sure of the way to translate the goal of making their organizations more intellectual into a strategic action

(Yang et al., 2009). Based on above and other concepts, Yang et al. (2009) identify to develop theoretically sound model namely organizational knowledge creation strategy. They were identified four dimensions of organizational knowledge creations strategies which may impact its knowledge asset. The organizational knowledge asset means the increment of knowledge storage through recombination of existing knowledge (Nonaka et al., 2000). Moreover, knowledge asset in the organizations includes the personnel's know-how, and organizational routines have evolved uniquely in each organization (Nonaka et al., 2000; Yang et al., 2009). Yang et al. (2009) were made up four dimensions, and distinguished between them can yield important insights. Especially, they noted that those four dimensions (exploration, institutional entrepreneurship, combination, exploitation) comprise the organizational knowledge creation strategies construct as demonstrated at EICE model. All four dimensions officially defined by Yang et al. (2009). In this research, we used the organizational knowledge creation strategy including four dimensions of exploration, institutional entrepreneurship, combination and exploitation.

The knowledge creation strategy dimensions of exploration defined are the process of converting new private knowledge through firm-specific unique knowledge. It is also a strategy for an organization to increase its intellectual capital by creating its unique private knowledge within its organizational boundary (Ichijo, 2002). Since the unique private knowledge must be valuable, rare, difficult for competitor to imitate, and difficult to imitate (Barney, 1991), new private knowledge can be acquired through discover and research existing private knowledge by the organizations themselves. Exploration includes knowledge created by terms such as search, innovation, discovery, flexibility, play, experimentation and risk taking (March, 1991). Exploration may also occur in innovation that is filled with new private knowledge, which is created by fusing together previously separate private knowledge (Yang et al., 2009).

Institutional entrepreneurship strategies are the process of articulating private knowledge into public knowledge. It also represents the activities of actors who have an interest in particular institutional arrangement and who leverage resource to transform existing institution or to create new ones (McGuire et al., 2004). When private knowledge is transformed publicly, knowledge is institutionalized, thus allowing it to be exploited by members in organizational field, it becomes the basis of new private knowledge creation (Yang et al., 2009). The successful conversion of private knowledge into public knowledge depends on three sets of critical activities: (1) the occupation of "subject position" that bridge diverse stakeholders and have wide legitimacy, (2) the theorization of new practices through discursive and political means, (3) the institutionalization of these new private knowledge by connecting them to stakeholders' routine and values (McGuire et al., 2004).

The strategy dimensions of combination are the process of converting public knowledge into more complex and advanced sets of public knowledge. It also represents the synthesis and application of current and acquired public knowledge (Kogut & Zander, 1992; Nahapiet & Ghoshal, 1998). While public knowledge includes knowledge not unique to any one firm and also exists in outside environment, combination occurs in the integration and configuration of public knowledge collected from outside or inside the organizations to form new public knowledge (Yang et al., 2009).

Exploitation strategies are the process of transforming public knowledge into firm-specific private knowledge. It also means enhancing the intellectual capital of a firm with existing public knowledge (Ichijo, 2002). Public knowledge is the technical sort shared in engineering drawings, research reports, conference publications, consulting manuals, textbooks and classrooms; it generally represents easily available technical solutions in the market. It is also tacit knowledge or social explicit knowledge with the potential of becoming social in easily documented forms (Matusik & Hill, 1998). For example, lean manufacturing, just-in-time inventory, total quality management and team-based incentives are "best practices" now in the public domain. Exploitation occurs when an organization accumulates knowledge from outside its boundaries and integrates this knowledge into organization-specific private knowledge (Yang et al., 2009). Exploitation does not mean the firm using existing knowledge just as it is. It is based on how to make better use of existing knowledge and the analysis in which we examine this public knowledge (Ichijo, 2002).

2.5.3 *Technology*

In the twenty-first century, innovation and technological progress will play a central role in both national and global economic development. Koh (2006) provided an economy that advances to the global technological frontier and narrows the technological gap, an innovation-based growth strategy that focuses on investment in R&D and technology creation offers the greatest potential for economic growth.

Most people have little difficulty expressing some notion of what it is for technology. For instance, technology is science plus purpose. While science is the study of laws of nature, technology is the practical application of those laws toward the achievement of some purposes. One may define technology as the organization of knowledge for the achievement of practical purpose. A more expanded definition of the term is a use of devices and systematic patterns of thought and activity to control physical and biological phenomena in order to serve man's desires with a minimum of resources and a maximum of efficiency. From another point, technology refers to the application of science to industrial and commercial objectives (Dorf, 2001). It is clear that science and technology are woven throughout a larger complex of human activity which is oriented around a mix of economic, political, humanitarian, and cultural means and ends (Custer, 1995). Moreover, others consider technology to be the machines, processes, methods, materials, tools and devices applied to industrial and commercial objectives. Most descriptions of technology noted that the primary uses of technology are industrial and commercial. Specialized descriptions of technology often focus on military, health, and safety objectives. Therefore, while there are many different descriptions of technology, finding the most useful one depends on addressing current challenges.

Typically, the technological resources of an organization encompass all of the equipment, machinery and systems (including the library, information systems hardware and software) that are essential for the organization to function properly (Lusthaus et al., 2002). In the early literature, Mitcham (1979) has outlined a useful four-dimensional framework for conceptualizing the term technology. This includes technology as: (a) artifact (tools, manufactured objects, etc.), (b) knowledge (scientific, engineering, uniquely technological how to knowledge, as well as insight from the social and physical sciences), (c) process (problem-solving, research & development, invention, innovation, etc.) and (d) volition (ethics, technology as a social construction, technology as a social force, etc.). It has clarified by Custer (1995) to explore each of these dimensions in turn as well as to discuss some implications for technology education. The traditional view of artifacts has focused almost exclusively on physical objects. These have been of two major types. The first, artifacts have been designed to extend human capability for some useful or productive purpose. For example, a microscope greatly extends the capability of the naked human eye. In general terms, this has to do with the history of tool development, or more broadly, the making of physical objects by human beings. The second dimension has to do with outcomes (products or made objects). Viewed historically, this includes a vast array of artifacts, from empire's pottery to musical instruments of the ancient world to the printed pages of the renaissance to modern rockets and satellites. The important point is that technological artifacts can appropriately and correctly be understood as the outcomes or products derived from the systematic application of rules to some process Typically, it may defined its technology as the tools, techniques and actions used to transform organizational inputs into outputs (Daft, 1988 cited by Custer, 1995). On reflection, it should also be obvious that a logical extension of the systematic approach includes management structures as artifacts, in effect blurs the distinction between technology as artifact and technology as process. Nevertheless, a conceptual distinction between process and artifact persists. Through continued use, testing, modification and refinement, processes begin to assume varying degrees of formality and structure. Rules, laws and documented procedures begin to emerge and receive the sanction of a community of practitioners. As this formalization occurs, processes become artifacts.

In today's information economy, rapid access to knowledge is critical to the success of many organizations. An information and communication technology (ICT) infrastructure provides a broad platform for exchanging data, coordinating activities, sharing information, emerging private and public sectors, and supporting globalization commerce, all based on powerful computing and network technology (Liao, 2003). Researchers agreed that within knowledge management (KM), maturity and the use of information technology (IT) development facilitates new methods and applications (such as groupware, on-line databases, intranets); it allows firms to deliver products and services better in quality and thus to achieve competitive advantage and profit (Shera & Lee, 2004). Sharing knowledge and information is an important factor in any organizations, thus several researchers concluded that ICT enables knowledge management activities for collaborative decision support, information sharing, organizational learning and organizational memory (Liao, 2003). Similarly, for R&D organizations, technology transfer is the process by which science and technology are transferred from one individual or group to another that incorporates this new knowledge into its way of doing things.

A new technology has a considerable relative advantage and has to provide significant value to the customer before it is embraced by the wider user community (Jain & Triandis, 1997). In utilizing new technology, there are numerous management challenges such as continuous improvement of technology is the basis of the future competitive advantage for a firm. Current management interests are also focused on knowledge management and IT as a major determinant of business excellence and competitive advantage.

Similarly, Shera and Lee (2004) investigated whether knowledge management (KM) and IT contribute to enhancing dynamic capabilities and, consequently, to improving business excellence and competitive advantage. Moreover, its empirical study, based on results from a survey of major Taiwanese firms, their study identified that both endogenous and exogenous knowledge through IT applications significantly enhances dynamic capabilities. Especially, they concluded to give implications that firms ought to give particular attention to KM in order to enhance dynamic capabilities to the end of out-competing rivals in a turbulent environment; and development of internet and database technology will facilitate more advanced IT applications in business administration and thus help to ensure excellence and competitiveness. In addition, the influence of KM was also found to be controlled by specific IT applications (Shera & Lee, 2004). From another point, advanced IT applications and network systems facilitate employee knowledge sharing; employees are the main drivers of knowledge and information sharing in organizations (Nonaka, 1994). Alavi and Leidner (2001) suggested that IT increases knowledge transfer by extending an individual's reach beyond formal lines of communication. For example, computer networks, electronic bulletin boards, intranets and database, and so on (Kim & Lee, 2006). Since technology is multifaceted, the organization must invest in a comprehensive infrastructure that supports the various types of knowledge and communication that are critical (Gold et al., 2001). Liao (2003) conducted an investigation using a classification of articles from 1995 to 2002, indexed by keywords, to explore how KM technologies and applications developed during that period. His study points out that information computing provides powerful information processing capabilities, while networking offers standards and connectivity for digital integration. Internet is a kind of ICT that combines with some other network technologies and services, such as intranet, extranet, virtual private network (VPN) and wireless web, to construct a digital environment to consistently create new knowledge, quickly disseminate it, and embody it in organizations (Liao, 2003).

Gold et al. (2001) defined that technology refers to the crucial element of the structural dimension needed to mobilize social capital for the creation of knowledge. Moreover, they identified technological dimensions that are part of effective knowledge management including business intelligence, collaboration, distributed learning, knowledge discovery, knowledge mapping, opportunity generation, as well as security. In developing an effective knowledge management, it is important to understand stages of ICT and fundamental issues and factors affecting adoption or rejection of technologies. The technical systems within an R&D organization determine how knowledge transfers or travels throughout the challenging project and knowledge is accessed.

Collaboration technologies and distributed learning technologies allow individuals within the organization to work together and collaborate interactively. Collaboration is seen as one of the key manners in which knowledge is transmitted and created within the organization (Gold, 2001). Knowledge discovery technologies allow an organization to search for new knowledge that is either internal or external. Knowledge mapping technologies allow an organization to track its sources of internal and external knowledge so that individuals in need of a specific type of knowledge know where it resides. Knowledge application technologies enable an organization to use its existing knowledge. Opportunity generation technologies allow an organization to generate and store knowledge about its customers, partners, employees, or suppliers (Gold et al., 2001). Finally, the effective technology transfer increases user involvement in the innovation process, which, in turn, positively affects R&D productivity and has long-term benefits in terms of funding support from the sponsor groups. Custer summarized that technology is indeed conceptually complex and multi-dimensional. It exists in many forms including artifact and knowledge, and process. In these various forms, it is woven into the very fabric of cultures around the world. As such, technology exercises profound influence within societies, institutions, governments, economies and much more. In this study, we chose to use the five dimensions of technology, namely collaboration technology, distributed learning technology, knowledge mapping technology and knowledge transfer technology which were developed by Gold et al. (2001) and artifact technology which was early suggested by Daft (1988) and later developed by Custer (1995).

2.5.4 *Human Resource Development*

Human resources management involves practices that ensure organizations' human capital (i.e., employees' knowledge, skills and abilities) contribute to business outcomes (Huselid et al., 1997). The theoretical literature suggests that human resource management increases productivity by increasing employees' skills and motivation (Huselid, 1995). Many organizations are highly dependent on their human capital to competitive advantage. Their market value increasingly depends on their intangible assets, such as their knowledge, core competencies and organizational capabilities (Lawler, 2005). According to the resource-based view, organizations attempt to exploit distinct competencies that are under their control in order to sustain a competitive advantage and these competencies can include facilities, monetary resources and human capital (Barney, 1991). Moreover, resource-based view suggests that human resource systems can contribute to sustained competitive advantage through facilitating the development of competencies that are firm specific, produce complex social relationships, are embedded in a firm's history and culture, and generate tacit organizational knowledge (Lado & Wilson, 1994). Human resource development refers to the practices used for enhancing employee skills through training and other forms of knowledge and skill enhancement (Lepak & Snell, 1999). Therefore, human resource development improves the human capital that people bring with them to the organization. To achieve a competitive advantage, organization need to generate specific knowledge because specific resources are unique and difficult to imitate (Barney, 1991). One way to generate firm-specific resources is human capital development (Lepak & Snell, 1999).

Rauch et al. (2005) explored about how three different human resource variables affect employment growth of small-scale enterprises: human capital of business owners, human capital of employees, and human resource development and utilization. Their study identified that business owners provided support for a main effect model indicating that owners' human capital as well as employee human resource development and utilization affect employment growth. Importantly, they point out that human resources development and utilization was most effective when the human capital of employees was high and they concluded that human resources are important factors in predicting the growth of small-scale enterprises. In addition, Rauch et al. (2005) defined four dimensions to HRD such as training and development of employees, decision-making involvement, support for personal initiative and goal communication and it was early suggested by Lepak and Snell (1999). Training and development of employees are important because the organization is not likely to find specific and unique skills in the labor market (Lepak & Snell, 1999). Therefore, these skills need to be developed internally. Additionally, employee development helps to shape employees' behavior and attitudes in such a way to make them consistent with organizational goals. Decision-making involvement helps to create ongoing commitment from employees, which in turn affects performance (Arthur, 1994; Huselid et al., 1997; Lepak & Snell, 1999). Support for personal initiative can be seen as an attempt of empowering employees because personal initiative describes extra role behaviors such as having more responsibility, working independently, and controlling one's own work independently. Empowering employees is also related to business outcomes (Arthur, 1994; Huselid et al., 1997). Goal setting is a main motivator in organizational settings and predicts performance (Locke & Latham, 1990). The goal of communication is to provide information to a person or group in a fashion which enables the person or group to integrate the new information with their own knowledge and to use it in making decisions. Moreover, Baum et al.'s (1998) empirical study identified that the effects of goals are partially mediated by goal communication.

The fundamental importance of HRD is found in the theory of human capital. The main assertion of the theory is that people possess skills, experience and knowledge that have economic value in an organization. The theory was originally developed in the context of the economic value of education, measured by expenditure and return on investment (Sparkes & Miyake, 2000). From another point, the theory of human capital supports the use of closely monitored training as the best way to assimilate knowledge transfer and many researchers have emphasized the importance of human resource management (HRM) as a way to improve the transfer of knowledge, especially in the form of technological know-how. For instance, Sparkes and Miyake's (2000) study identified the appropriate emphases in HRD practices that enhance the transfer of knowledge. Moreover, there are a number of human resource management patterns that a firm can employ in order to enhance knowledge transfer. The patterns to be chosen depend on the type of production operation and business strategy the firm adopts. The analysis demonstrates that there are obvious patterns to be avoided if a firm desires to secure the maximum benefits from its HRD efforts (Sparkes & Miyake, 2000). In addition, recently studies argued that the organizational performance and growth are dependent on successful human resource development management in terms of enhancing motivation, performance, involvement loyalty and commitment (Sharabi & Harpaz, 2010). They (Sharabi & Harpaz, 2010) also identified that the concept "work centrality" refers to the degree of general importance that work has in an individual's life at any given time, since high work centrality is positively related to the above advantages such as motivation, performance involvement loyalty and commitment. The most interesting finding of their study is among those who did not experience expressive work events; there was a meaningful decrease of work centrality so that eventually their work centrality was much lower than those who did experience expressive work events. Work centrality tends to increase over the course of life. Moreover, they noted that maintaining high work centrality is related to various positive organizational outcomes. Hence, maintaining high work centrality and promoting work centrality should have positive consequences on organizational performance and effectiveness (Sharabi & Harpaz, 2010). It means we also need to consider work centrality because it can have positive consequences on organizational effectiveness and from another way, it is also much related to employees experience expressive work events its HRD. Finally, the high investment in training and development programs, promotions planning, job enrichment and work design, and other HRD activities have to have proven effective outcomes related to an organization's core competencies and human capital (Blackman & Lee-Kelley, 2006). Overall, this study used the dimensions of training and development of employees, decision-making involvement, personal initiative and goal of communication for measure to assessing HRD due to significance of the study.

2.5.5 Interrelationships Among Variables

Research has illuminated various interrelations among the variables. The following sections explicate the interrelations among variables of organizational culture, strategy, technology, HRD, knowledge management, transformational leadership and organizational effectiveness.

2.5.6 Organizational Culture, Knowledge Management and Organizational Effectiveness

The study applies the culture framework developed by Denison and his colleagues (Denison, 1990; Denison & Mishra, 1995; Denison, et al., 2003; Fey & Denison, 2003) which is very essential to the relationship between organizational culture and effectiveness. Denison and his colleagues (Denison, 1990; Denison & Mishra, 1995; Denison et al., 2003) identified and validated four dimensions of organizational cultures; involvement, consistency, adaptability and mission. Typically, Denison et al.'s (Denison, 1990; Denison et al., 2003) two dimensions, namely involvement and adaptability, are indicators of flexibility, openness and responsiveness, and were strong predictors of growth. The other two dimensions, consistency and mission, are indicators of integration, direction and vision, and were better predictors of profitability. Each of the four dimensions was also significant predictors of other effectiveness criteria such as quality, employee satisfaction and overall performance (Denison & Mishra, 1995). Many studies raise the issue of organizational culture's influence on knowledge management success. However, few investigate how this influence manifests itself or examine the specific relationship between organizational culture and knowledge management, Gold et al.'s (2001) research review of the cultural environment conductive to knowledge management suggested that shaping culture is central in a firm's ability to manage its knowledge more effectively. At any organization the interaction between individuals is essential in the innovation process. For example, dialogues between individuals or groups are often the basis for the creation of new ideas; therefore, it can be viewed as potential for creating knowledge. Moreover, Turban and Aronson (2001) emphasize that the ability of an organization to learn, develop memory and share knowledge is dependent on its culture. While contemporary literature provides numerous examples of knowledge management (KM) success stories, firms seeking to engage in such efforts also face a variety of challenges. Among the most difficult of these challenges is organizational culture. Regarding this challenge, Janz and Prasarnphanich (2003) emphasized that "Organizational culture is believed to be the most significant input to effective KM and organizational learning in that corporate culture determines values, beliefs, and work systems that could encourage or impede knowledge creation and sharing" (Alavi et al., 2005). The above and other concepts lead to the hypothesis: H1: organizational culture (adaptability, consistency, mission and involvement) is positively affected to its knowledge management; H2: organizational culture (adaptability, consistency, mission and involvement) is positively affected to its organizational effectiveness; H3: knowledge management is a mediator between organizational culture and organizational effectiveness.

2.5.7 *Organizational Strategy, Knowledge Management and Organizational Effectiveness*

Organizational strategy refers to the pattern or plan that integrates an organization's major goals, policies and action sequence into a cohesive whole, it is the high level long-term meta-plan by which the ultimate success and viability of an organization (Quinn, 1980). Organizational strategy is particularly important for research organizations due to many uncertainties and need to coordinate disparate activities to meet organizational goals and objectives. Moreover, organizational strategic plan can provide a mechanism for focusing on future needs and staying in tune with fundamental organizational priorities and goals (Jain & Triandis, 1997). If knowledge and its creation process are so important a determinant of organizational performance, then knowledge creation strategies are likely to be a key area of strategic choice for the organization (Yang et al., 2009). Indeed, organizational knowledge creation is the capability of an organization as a whole to create new knowledge, disseminate it throughout the organizational and embody it in products, services and systems (Nonaka & Takeuchi, 1995). While the dynamic perspective on knowledge that emphasizes how new knowledge leads to generation of new organizational outcomes is also evoked by knowledge management researchers (Kogut & Zander, 1992; Nonaka & Takeuchi, 1995), many scholars develop to classify and define organizational strategy with different points. For example, Yang and his colleagues' (2009) study identified four dimensions of knowledge creation strategies (EICE: exploration, institutional entrepreneurship, combination, exploitation) in organizational setting and have clarified the relationship between the organization's knowledge creation strategies and knowledge asset. Those above dimensions of organizational knowledge creation strategies are described as follows: exploration strategies describe firms using formal or informal integrating mechanisms to stimulate the creation of new private firm-specific knowledge and to facilitate the transfer existing private knowledge to different areas of the firm. Institutional entrepreneurship is the strategic activities of actors who have an interest in particular institutional arrangement and who leverage resource to transform existing institution or to create new ones. Combination is the strategic activities of the integration and configuration of public knowledge collected from outside or inside the organizations to form new public knowledge. Moreover, exploitation is the strategic activities for enhancing the intellectual capital of a firm with existing public knowledge. Their study achieved the organizational knowledge creation strategies that significantly impacted its knowledge assets. In the knowledge-based century, it may be more appropriate organization strategy using any area of contemporary organizations. Thus, the above and other concepts lead to the hypothesis: H4: organizational strategy (exploration, institutional entrepreneurship, combination and exploitation) is positively affected to its knowledge management; H5: organizational strategy (exploration, institutional entrepreneurship, combination and exploitation) is positively affected to organizational effectiveness; H6: knowledge management is a mediator between organizational strategy and organizational effectiveness.

2.5.8 Technology, Knowledge Management and Organizational Effectiveness

Technology is indeed conceptually complex and multi-dimensional. It exists in many forms including artifact, knowledge and process. In these various forms, it is woven into the very fabric of cultures around the world. As such, technology exercises profound influence within societies, institutions, governments, economies and much more (Custer, 1995). Basically, technology refers to the systems of the organization that allow the capture, flow, access, produce and use of knowledge through the enterprise (Smith, 2006). Artifact technology may refer as the tools, techniques and actions used to transform organizational inputs into outputs. For example, in R&D organization it may include laboratory equipment, instrument which is need to analyze research results. Organizations can create a competitive advantage by using information technology to create a positive work environment. Scholars agreed that new method and applications of IT development facilitates (such as groupware, on-line databases, intranets) allow firms to deliver better quality' product and services and thus firm's to achieve competitive advantage and profit (Shera & Lee, 2004). Gold and his colleagues

(2001) identified several dimensions of technology which is related to effective knowledge management as well as the following: collaboration, distributed learning, knowledge discovery, knowledge mapping, knowledge application and opportunity generation. However, some dimensions were dropped in other empirical studies (Smith, 2006). Based on the above and other literature reviews, this study embedded five dimensions (artifact technology, collaboration technology, distributed learning technology, knowledge mapping technology and knowledge transfer [sharing] technology) on the hypothesized model. Therefore, it was hypothesized that: H7: technology (artifact technology, collaboration technology, distributed learning technology, knowledge mapping technology and knowledge transfer technology) is positively affected to its knowledge management; H8: technology (artifact technology, collaboration technology, distributed learning technology, knowledge mapping technology and knowledge transfer technology) is positively affected to its organizational effectiveness; H9: knowledge management is a mediator between technology and organizational effectiveness.

2.5.9 Human Resource Development, Knowledge Management and Organizational Effectiveness

Human resource development (HRD) refers to the practices used for enhancing employee skills through training and other forms of knowledge and skill enhancement (Lepak & Snell, 1999). Therefore, human resource development improves the human capital that people bring with them to the organization. Rauch and his colleagues (2005) defined four dimensions to human resource development and utilization: training and development of employees, decision-making involvement, support for personal initiative and goal communication. In addition, we add the dimension of "work centrality" to the measure and assessment of HRD in this study. The theory of human capital supports the use of closely monitored training as the best way to assimilate knowledge transfer. Many organizations are highly dependent on their human capital competitive advantage and their market value increasingly depends on their intangible assets, such as their knowledge, core competencies and organizational capabilities (Lawler, 2005). Moreover, several researchers argued that the organizational performance and growth are dependent on successful human resource development management in terms of enhancing motivation, performance, involvement loyalty and commitment (Sharabi & Harpaz, 2010). Therefore, based on above and other literature reviews leading to hypothesized that: H10: human resource development (training & development, decision-making involvement, support for personal initiative and goal of communication) is positively affected to its knowledge management; H11: human resource development (training & development, decision-making involvement, support for personal initiative and goal of communication) is positively affected to its organizational effectiveness; H12: knowledge management is a mediator between human resource development and organizational effectiveness.

2.5.10 Knowledge Management and Organizational Effectiveness

The knowledge management is usually analyzed from a process perspective. Many frameworks for the process have been identified. This study examines four processes that have received the most consensuses: knowledge creation (acquisition), sharing (conversion), utilization (application) and protection. Creation-oriented knowledge management processes are toward obtaining knowledge. The creation (acquisition) process refers to the organization's effort to gather information and new knowledge from internal and external sources and codify it into explicit knowledge (Lee & Sukoco, 2007). Innovation, another aspect of creation, is the generation of new knowledge from the application of existing knowledge. The creation of organizational knowledge requires the sharing and dissemination (i.e., collaboration) of personal experiences (Andrew & Dinur, 1998). Knowledge sharing process means the exchange of knowledge and share of experience among different individual, groups and organizations (Davenport & Prusak, 1998). Knowledge utilization refers to the process that is oriented toward the actual use of knowledge (Gold et al., 2001). Protection has not been frequently studied, but must be included to signify the extreme importance knowledge holds with regard to the competitive advantage of an organization. Therefore, knowledge protection process refers to protect the knowledge from inappropriate or illegal use or from theft (Gold et al., 2001).

Knowledge management capabilities are associated with organizational effectiveness in management literature (Davenport & Prusak, 1998; Nonaka & Takeuchi, 1995). For example, through knowledge creation, the insights of individuals are converted into knowledge that can be used to design new products or improve performance. Knowledge management has been regarded as contributing to enhancing organizational effectiveness. The findings of empirical study imply that knowledge management processes are significant predictors for organizational creativity and business organizations can achieve strategic and economic benefits of knowledge management by utilizing organizational creativity in an effective fashion (Lee & Choi, 2000). In addition, more and more people agree that this knowledge base is a valuable firm asset, and that enlarging the knowledge base and improving its use will contribute to the effectiveness of the R&D process (Meyers & Wilemon, 1989; Takeuchi & Nonaka, 1986). Drongelen et al. (1996) observed that, as R&D processes are in essence information transformation processes, knowledge accumulation and dissemination activities are in fact embedded in the mainstream R&D process. Also, knowledge management is largely based on mechanisms, such as multifunctional project teams, which are also aimed at other purposes (e.g., improving quality or speeding up the R&D process). Based on these and other studies, it was hypothesized in this study that: H13: knowledge management (knowledge creation, knowledge sharing, knowledge utilization and knowledge protection) is positively affected to its organizational effectiveness.

2.5.11 *Transformational Leadership, Knowledge Management and Organizational Effectiveness*

Previous research has demonstrated that transformational leadership appears to be an effective style for use in R&D settings (Elkins & Keller, 2003; Keller et al., 1992) and their study gives a proposition about leadership in the R&D context that transformational leadership in research project will be positively related to project effectiveness. In addition, Berson and Linton (2005) clarified that transformational leadership includes intellectual stimulation consisting of encouraging creativity and change in followers, and individualized consideration that implies paying attention to individual needs and the continuous facilitation of their development and it has indicated that transformational leadership tends to support quality as well as satisfaction in R&D environments. Choo's (1996) research identified the insights of individuals who are converted into knowledge that can be used to design new products or improve performance. Crawford and his colleagues' series of articles (Crawford, 2005; Crawford & Strohkirch, 2000; Crawford et al., 2003) found that transformational leadership is significantly related to innovation outcomes, as innovation involves the ability to create and manage information and knowledge. Moreover, innovation is also often assumed to be one of the important characteristics of knowledge managers. Crawford's (2005) recently research emphasized that transformational leaders are better suited to handle even the most technical aspects of the modern workplace than transactional or laissez-faire leaders. Additionally, as individual leaders move up in an organization they are better suited to engage in knowledge management, because they are more transformational in leadership style. The above and other concepts lead to the hypothesis: H14: transformational leadership (idealized attributes, idealized influence, inspirational motivation, intellectual stimulation and individualized consideration) positively affected to organizational effectiveness; H15: transformational leadership is a moderator in the relationship between knowledge management and organizational effectiveness.

2.6 Summary

The literature review provided a theoretical basis for the research hypothesized model. Three main theories were explored as organizational-based view, knowledge-based view and resource-based view as well as the interdependency among the theoretical paradigms highlighted. Organizational effectiveness was discussed within the context of goal approach. Knowledge management was presented along definitional lines of the process of knowledge creation, conversion (sharing), utilization and protection. Transformational leadership was presented along definition of the behavioral components of idealized attributes, idealized influence, inspirational motivation, intellectual stimulation and individualized consideration which was originally developed by Bass and Avolio (1990a, 1990b). In addition, organizational culture, organizational strategy, technology and human resource development constructs were respectably highlighted through many different and important literatures developed by different authors. Moreover, a brief overview was also presented in the R&D literature review due to interesting of objective area.

CHAPTER 3

Systematic Path to Problem Solving

Abstract This chapter details the research methodology, defining the primary variables and presenting the research model and hypotheses. Organizational effectiveness is the dependent variable, while organizational culture, strategy, technology and human resource development (HRD) are independent variables. Knowledge management functions as a mediating variable and transformational leadership serves as a moderating variable. The chapter explains the development of hypotheses based on research questions and literature review. It describes the definitions of factors, data collection procedures, experimental tests and data analysis methods, including regression and hierarchical regression analyses, to evaluate the impact of these variables on organizational effectiveness.

Keywords Knowledge management · Transformational leadership · Organizational effectiveness · Mediator · Moderator · Organizational culture · Organizational strategy · Technology · Human resource development

B. Dorjgotov, *Enhancing Organizational Effectiveness Through Knowledge Management and Transformational Leadership*,
https://doi.org/10.1007/978-981-97-8039-6_3

3.1 Introduction

The purpose of this study is to examine the impacts among organizational culture, strategy, technology, HRD, knowledge management, transformational leadership and organizational effectiveness using a hypothesis model in R&D-based organization. Especially, the study aimed to explore the mediating effects of knowledge management in the relationship between organizational culture, strategy, technology, HRD and organizational effectiveness; the moderating effect of transformational leadership on knowledge management and organizational effectiveness. The study survey includes a sample of 524 R&D professionals at 21 research institutes of Mongolian Academy of Sciences using the purposive sampling method. A survey was utilized to collect data on participants' perceptions of their organizational culture, strategy, technology, HRD, knowledge management, transformational leadership and organizational effectiveness. Demographic, regression and hierarchical regression analysis was used to examine the weight among variables and as well as the tool for addressing research questions. The regression and hierarchical regression analysis allows researcher to assess "the contribution of each scale (variable) items as well as incorporate how well the scale measures the concept on the relationship between dependent, independent, mediating and moderating variables."

3.2 Constitutive Definition

There are seven major concepts in this study: organizational effectiveness, knowledge management, transformational leadership, organizational culture, organizational strategy, technology and human resource development. The following paragraphs define these seven concepts as used in this study.

Organizational effectiveness refers to the extent to which an organization is able to fulfill its goals (Lusthaus et al., 2002).

Knowledge management refers as "the overall task of managing the process of knowledge creation (acquisition), conversion, utilization and protection, as well as the related activities."

Transformational leadership is a leader's behavior as "those who motivate their followers to perform beyond expectation by raising the follower's confidence levels and providing support for developing high levels" (Burns, 1978).

Organizational culture refers as "a pattern of basic assumptions, invented, discovered, or developed by a given group, as it learns to cope with its problems of external adaptation and internal integration, that has worked well enough to be considered valid and, therefore is to be taught to new members as the correct way to perceive, think, and feel in relation to those problems" (Schein, 1988).

Organizational strategy refers as "the pattern or plan that integrates an organization's major goals, policies and action sequence into a cohesive whole, it is the high level long-term meta-plan by which the ultimate success and viability of an organization" (Quinn, 1980).

Technology refers to "the systems of the organization that allow the capture, flow, access and use of knowledge and as well as the tools, techniques and actions used to transform organizational inputs into outputs" (Custer, 1995; Daft, 1988; Smith, 2006).

Human resource development refers to "the practices used for enhancing employee skills through training and other forms of knowledge and skill enhancement" (Lepak & Snell, 1999).

3.3 Research Design

The study utilizes the sample regression analysis technique to explore the contribution of:

1. Organizational culture related to its knowledge management,
2. Organizational culture related to its organizational effectiveness,
3. Organizational strategy related to its knowledge management,
4. Organizational strategy related to its organizational effectiveness
5. Technology related to its knowledge management,
6. Technology related to its organizational effectiveness,
7. Human resource development related to its knowledge management,
8. Human resource development related to its organizational effectiveness.

Regression and hierarchical regression analysis will also examine:

1. the mediating effect of knowledge management between organizational culture and organizational effectiveness

2. the mediating effect of knowledge management between organizational strategy and organizational effectiveness
3. the mediating effect of knowledge management between technology and organizational effectiveness
4. the mediating effect of knowledge management between HRD and organizational effectiveness
5. the moderating effect of transformational leadership on both knowledge management and organizational effectiveness.

3.4 Research Model and Hypotheses

In the research model, organizational effectiveness is dependent variable and organizational culture, organizational strategy, technology and human resource development are independent variables, knowledge management is mediator variable and transformational leadership is a moderator variable. There are number of possible hypotheses that could be developed from the research questions and the literature review. The 15 hypotheses relating to the streams of research in organizational culture, strategy, technology, HRD, knowledge management, transformational leadership and organizational effectiveness were considered for testing (see Fig. 3.1).

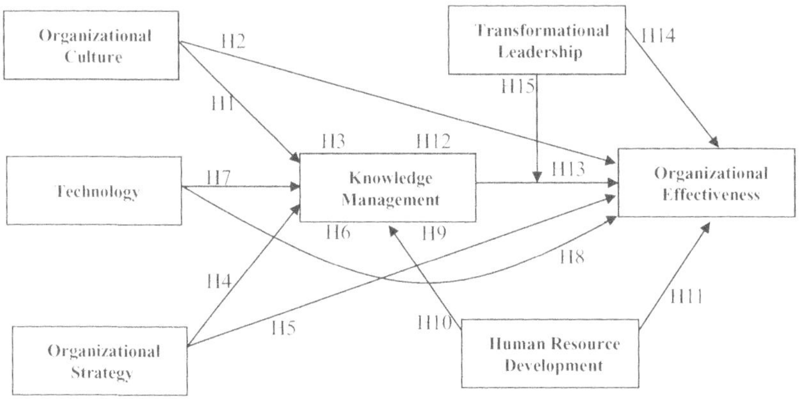

Fig. 3.1 Research model

H1: organizational culture is positively affected to its knowledge management.
H2: organizational culture is positively affected to its organizational effectiveness.
H3: knowledge management is a mediator between organizational culture and organizational effectiveness.
H4: organizational strategy is positively affected to its knowledge management.
H5: organizational strategy is positively affected to organizational effectiveness.
H6: knowledge management is a mediator between organizational strategy and organizational effectiveness.
H7: technology is positively affected to its knowledge management.
H8: technology is positively affected to its organizational effectiveness.
H9: knowledge management is a mediator between technology and organizational effectiveness.
H10: human resource development is positively affected to its knowledge management.
H11: human resource development is positively affected to its organizational effectiveness.
H12: knowledge management is a mediator between human resource development and organizational effectiveness.
H13: knowledge management is positively affected to its organizational effectiveness.
H14: transformational leadership positively affected to organizational effectiveness.
H15: transformational leadership is a moderator between knowledge management and organizational effectiveness

3.5 Instrument

A self administrated survey was used to collect data for variables of organizational effectiveness, culture, strategy, technology, HRD and knowledge management, transformational leadership. The research questionnaire was designed to obtain information specially needed to conduct this study and to measure the variables listed in the measurement section. The questionnaire utilized in this study was developed by the researcher to successfully achieve the objectives of the study.

The questionnaire was organized into two parts. The first part was variables of organizational effectiveness, knowledge management, transformational leadership, organizational culture, organizational strategy, technology and HRD. The second part was demographics (Appendix B). The questionnaire was developed by selecting and integrating questions used in previous research. Likert-type scales (1 = strongly agree, 2 = agree, 3 = slightly agree, 4 = neither agree or nor disagree, 5 = slightly disagree, 6 = disagree, 7 = strongly disagree) were used to measure the variables. The questionnaires contained 68 questions: 8 questions relating to organizational effectiveness, 8 questions relating to knowledge management, 10 questions relating to transformational leadership, 12 questions relating to organizational culture, 7 questions relating to organizational strategy, 8 questions relating to technology, 8 questions relating to HRD and 7 questions relating to individual information (demographic).

3.6 Measurement

Seven variables (organizational effectiveness, knowledge management, transformational leadership, organizational culture, organizational strategy, technology, HRD,) were identified for study. Survey questionnaires were adapted from existing items used in past research.

3.6.1 Organizational Effectiveness

Basically, organizational effectiveness refers to the extent to which an organization is able to fulfill its goals (Lusthaus et al., 2002). Items (questionnaires) capturing organizational effectiveness were adopted from Gold's et al. (2001) items that measure three dimensions of effectiveness: efficiency, adaptability and innovations. Moreover, researcher add some items relating to specials of number of patent obtained and publication which are arguable characteristics of effectiveness in an R&D organization. Because, in an R&D organization, many units of output are intangible and subjective in nature, therefore, it seems in pure research the publication criterion is weighted more heavily, and applied research

Table 3.1 Organizational effectiveness scale

No	*Questions*
1	Our organization's ability to obtain more research fund is improving
2	Our organization has improved its ability to increase the number of reports, publication and new products
3	Our organization has improved its ability to increase the number of received patent
4	Our organization has improved its ability to quickly adapt its aim and goals to industry/market changes
5	Our organization has improved its ability to adjust individuals goals are consistent organizational goals
6	Our organization has improved its ability to foresee risks and benefits
7	Our organization has improved its ability to innovate new products/services
8	Our organization has improved its ability to rapidly commercialize new innovations

is the product that has been invented. In this study, organizational effectiveness was measured with eight items on a 7-point scale, ranging from strongly agree (1) to strongly disagree (7). See Table 3.1.

3.6.2 Knowledge Management

Knowledge management refers to "the overall task of managing the process of knowledge creation (acquisition), conversion, utilization and protection, as well as the related activities." Items measure knowledge management effectiveness adopted from Gold et al. (2001).

Gold et al. (2001) developed items to measure how much the knowledge creation, conversion, utilization and protection processes are presented in an organization. Gold et al.'s (2001) scales were modified to measure each of four knowledge management processes. In this study, knowledge management was measured with 8 items on a 7-point scale, ranging from strongly agree (1) to strongly disagree (7). See Table 3.2.

3.6.3 Transformational Leadership

Transformational leadership is a leader's behavior as those who motivate their followers to perform beyond expectation by raising the follower's confidence levels and providing support for developing high levels (Burns, 1978). Bass and his colleagues' (Bass, 1985; Bass & Avolio,

Table 3.2 Knowledge management scale

No	*Questions*
1	Our organization acquires new knowledge from existing knowledge
2	Our organization generates knowledge about new product/services within our industry
3	Our organization has process for transferring organizational knowledge to individuals
4	Our organization has a process to absorb knowledge from individuals into organization
5	Our organization has process to apply knowledge learned from mistakes/experiences
6	Our organization has a process to improve their efficiency by using their knowledge
7	Our organization has a process to protect knowledge from inappropriate use inside the organization
8	Our organization has processes to protect knowledge from inappropriate use from outside the organization

1994, 1995) research expanded Burns's factors of leadership theory. They have identified five factors which the behavioral components of transformational leadership: idealized attributes, idealized influence, inspirational motivation, intellectual stimulation and individualized consideration.

Transformational leadership questionnaires adopted from the Multifactor Leadership Questionnaire (MLQ 5x-short) created by Bass and Avolio (1995) and measured with 12 items on a 7-point scale, ranging from strongly agree (1) to strongly disagree (7). See Table 3.3.

3.6.4 Organizational Culture

Organizational culture refers as "a pattern of basic assumptions, invented, discovered, or developed by a given group, as it learns to cope with its problems of external adaptation and internal integration, that has worked well enough to be considered valid and, therefore is to be taught to new members as the correct way to perceive, think, and feel in relation to those problems" (Schein, 1988). The properties of organizational culture include the dimensions of mission, adaptability, involvement and consistency. Items were adapted from Fey and Denision (2003), with contributions from Denison himself. Denison and his colleagues (Denison, 1990; Denison & Mishra, 1995; Fey & Denison, 2003) have

Table 3.3 Transformational leadership scale

No	*Questions*
1	Our organization's leader/manager instills pride in me for being associated with him/her
2	Our organization's leader/manager shows a sense of power and confidence
3	Our organization's leader/manager talks about our most important values and beliefs
4	Our organization's leader/manager specifies the importance of having a strong sense of purpose
5	Our organization's leader/manager talks optimistically about the future
6	Our organization's leader/manager talks enthusiastically about what needs to be accomplished
7	Our organization's leader/manager re-examines critical assumptions to question whether they are appropriate
8	Our organization's leader/manager suggests new ways to complete assignments
9	Our organization's leader/manager treats me as an individual rather than just as a member of a group
10	Our organization's leader/manager helps me to develop my ability

been developing and improving an instrument measuring organizational culture through series of empirical studies since 1990.

Due to large number of items employed in the previous study, there is 12 items that showed the highest factor loadings within each dimensions were selected, upon consultation with Denison and his colleagues. Thus, Denison and his colleagues' (Denison, 1990; Denison & Mishra, 1995; Fey & Denison, 2003) 36 items were reduced to 12 items to modify in the study. In this study, organizational culture was measured with 12 items on a 7-point scale, ranging from strongly agree (1) to strongly disagree (7). See Table 3.4.

3.6.5 Organizational Strategy

The organizational strategy is understood as the pattern or plan that integrates an organization's major goals, policies and action sequence into a cohesive whole, it is the high level long-term meta-plan by which the ultimate success and viability of an organization are defined (Quinn, 1980). Items capturing organizational strategy were adopted from Yang et al. (2009) scales that measures four dimensions of strategy: exploration, institutional entrepreneurship, combination and exploitation.

Table 3.4 Organizational culture scale

No	*Questions*
1	In our organization, information is widely shared so that everyone can get the information whenever he or she need
2	In our organization, people work like they are part of team
3	The capability of people in this organization is viewed as an main source of competitive advantage
4	If there are difficult issues or problems in our organization, we solve them simply
5	Our organization implements projects simply by involving their functional units of our organization
6	In our organization, there is a clear and consistent set of values in this organization that governs the way we do business
7	It's compatible for our organization to work in new and improved ways
8	In our organization customers' comments and recommendations often lead the changes of our organization
9	In our organization, we determine our activity and efforts by coordinating between different units of organization
10	In our organization there is a clear strategy for the future
11	In our organization, there is widespread agreement about goals of this organization
12	We share our thoughts about our organization's future

In this study, organizational strategy was measured with 7 items on a 7-point scale, ranging from strongly agree (1) to strongly disagree (7). See Table 3.5. Yang et al. (2009) developed items to measure how much the organizational strategy creating knowledge is presented in an organization because knowledge creation is very important in an contemporary organizations especially in an R&D-based organizations. Yang and his colleagues (2009) original items displayed high construct validity because all the factor loadings were above 0.75.

3.6.6 *Technology*

Technology refers to "the systems of the organization that allow the capture, flow, access and use of knowledge and as well as the tools, techniques and actions used to transform organizational inputs into outputs" (Custer, 1995; Daft, 1988; Smith, 2006). Scale measures five dimensions of technology: artifact technology, collaboration technology, distributed

Table 3.5 Organizational strategy scale

No	*Questions*
1	Our organization motivates a process to create a new private firm-specific knowledge by using formal or informal mechanisms
2	Our organization simplifies a process to shift private knowledge to different sectors by using formal or informal mechanism
3	Our organization has the strategic activities of people who have an interest in particular institutional arrangement
4	Our organization has the strategic activities of people who leverage resource to transform existing institution and create new ones
5	Our organization has a process to form new public knowledge by the integrated and configured public knowledge which is collected from outside of organization
6	Our organization has a process to form new public knowledge by the integrated and configured public knowledge which is collected from inside of organization
7	Our organization has a process increase intellectual capital by strategic activity with open public knowledge

learning technology, knowledge mapping technology and knowledge transfer technology. In this study, technology was measured with 8 items on a 7-point scale, ranging from strongly agree (1) to strongly disagree (7). Six of eight items capturing technology were adopted from Gold et al. (2001) study and two of eight items capturing based literature reviews which related to dimensions of artifact technology.

Artifact technology refers to the tools, techniques and actions used to transform organizational inputs into outputs, and it must be concerned the assessing of organizational technology. See Table 3.6.

3.6.7 Human Resource Development

Human resource development (HRD) refers to the practices used for enhancing employee skills through training and other forms of knowledge and skill enhancement (Lepak & Snell, 1999). Items measure assessing of HRD adopted from the study of Rauch and his colleagues (2005). Scale that measures four dimensions of HRD: training & development, decision making involvement, support for personal initiative and goal of communication. In this study, HRD was measured with 8 items on a 7-point scale, ranging from strongly agree (1) to strongly disagree (7). Cronbach's α of human resource development is 0.930. See Table 3.7.

Table 3.6 Technology scale

No	*Questions*
1	Our organization uses technology that allows the translation of scientific knowledge to into products or process
2	Our organization uses technology that allow practical application for achievement of my research propose
3	Our organization uses technology that as a possibility for employee to collaborate with other people of organization
4	Our organization uses technology as a possibility for employees to work at one time from different places or learn from one source as a team
5	Our organization uses technology as a possibility for employees to work at different places at different time or from different sources as a one team
6	Our organization uses technologies as a possibility to give chance to illustrate the location (i.e., an individual, specific system or database) of specific types of knowledge
7	Our organization uses technology as a possibility to share knowledge, information and experiences which is gained by my experience with individuals
8	Our organization uses technology as a possibility to collaborate with other employees by sharing information and knowledge

Table 3.7 Human resource development scale

No	*Questions*
1	Our organization has an opportunities to attend any course and training programs
2	Our organization supports as changes and desires to learn at work
3	Our organization employees say "work is important at any given time of my life"
4	Our organization has a process to support involvement of employees when there is a decision of work made
5	Our organization's employees are encouraged to take responsibility
6	Our organization's employees are encouraged to work independently, and to control their work themselves
7	Our organization has a communication process which is associated to working aim and goals
8	Our organization has a regular information process which is associated with development's aim and meetings, seminars

3.6.8 Demographics

Demographic information of gender, scientific field, number of employees, academic rank, length of working time and education level were gathered for descriptive purposes only. Furthermore, the demographic information of the sample data is present in Chapter 4 for the following: gender by scientific field environment, academic rank by scientific field environment, educational level by scientific field environment, and duration of the employment by scientific field environment.

3.7 Translation

The questionnaire used in this study was originally composed in English, but was translated into Mongolian and then translated back to English to ensure accuracy. To make the translation valid, the study formed a panel. This panel consisted of five members. Two of them were scientist at the Mongolian Academy of Sciences and they were obtained their doctor degree in USA and Australia. Two of them were doctoral degree candidates at University of Wisconsin-Madison and University of Pennsylvania, USA and one of them was a Mongolian professional translator. The panel discussed and translated each question into Mongolian. Then, to ensure a correct translation, it was translated back to English. Unclear and incorrect translations were discussed to establish more meaningful questions, and to create the final questionnaire in Mongolian.

3.8 Pilot Test

In order to improve the effectiveness of the measurement instrument, a reliability test of the Mongolia version of the questionnaire was conducted. The questionnaire was pre-tested at three stages. First, face validity was pre-tested. The dissertation committee members (advisors) from Nanhua University, who are knowledgeable in the literature and the process of questionnaire design, reviewed the questionnaire and commented on its clarity. Second, two international business experts (professors at National University of Mongolia) reviewed the questionnaire to comment on its clarity and relevance. Finally, it was pre-tested forty R&D professional who are working at Mongolian Academy of Science responded to the Mongolian questionnaire. This pre-test identified areas for possible misunderstandings and provided validity of the questionnaire. This pilot test process helped increase the face and content validity before conducting the actual research study. Following the pre-test with subjects, an internal consistency reliability coefficient (Cronbach's α) of each item was calculated using the SPSS statistical processing package. To determine the internal consistency of each question, the study looked at all of the items simultaneously, using coefficient α. The coefficient α, or Cronbach's, measured the degree to which instrument questions were homogeneous and reflected the same underlying construct. An acceptable level of internal consistency would be reflected in an α value of no less than 0.70 in this study. The results of the Cronbach's α showed that the questionnaire of each variable had relatively high coefficient α higher than 0.89. However, several modifications were made in the questionnaire based on the committee's comments and the results from the pilot-tests. The final result of the questionnaire is shown in Table 4.5.

3.9 Sampling Plan

The sampled population of this study consisted of R&D professionals from the Mongolian Academy of Sciences (MAS). The MAS was selected because it is the primary R&D organization in Mongolia, serving as the central institution and scientific think-tank dedicated to the development of science and advanced technology in the country. The R&D professionals represented in this study included engineers, researchers, scientists, and managers. Currently, the MAS operates 21 research institutes in both natural and social sciences. The proposed sampling method was employed in this study. All 21 organizations cooperated by distributing questionnaires directly to their respective research institutes. Questionnaires were collected three weeks later. Out of 750 distributed questionnaires, 552 responses were received. After excluding 28 incomplete responses, 524 valid responses were retained for data analysis, yielding an effective response rate of 69%.

3.10 Data Collection Procedures

The group administrated questionnaires survey used in the study. The research institutes of Mongolian Academy of Sciences (MAS) were asked to participate in the study, and questionnaires were directly sent to them with hard copy of questionnaires and collected questionnaires back. The survey took approximately one and half month due to research institutes of MAS locating in the different regions.

Data collection consisted of six steps. In the first step, related research variables were identified through the literature review, advice from experts and field experience. The second step involved the drafting of the sample questionnaire with the dissertation committee and experts. The third step was the translation of the questionnaire into the Mongolian language, which was then translated back into the English language to ensure accuracy. The fourth step was a pre-test of the Mongolian questionnaire. Following the pre-test, an internal consistency reliability coefficient of each question was calculated. The questionnaire was modified again as a result of this pre-test to achieve greater clarity. For the fifth step, both the Mongolian questionnaire and the English questionnaire were mailed to the Administration office of MAS, and to a manager (director, science secretary) who was in charge of the subsidiary in research institutes of MAS. These persons then assigned R&D professionals to complete the questionnaire. The R&D professionals could choose either the Mongolian version or the English version. However, almost all respondents used the Mongolian version questionnaire. A cover letter by Mongolian and Consent form in Mongolian and English (Appendix A) was attached with the questionnaire to inform the respondents for the objective, the significance and the usefulness of the research. The reason for sending the English version was to help those who didn't understand the Mongolian content of the questionnaire. Finally, the filled out questionnaires were back to the administration office of MAS from research institutes.

3.11 Data Analysis

The data of this study were analyzed using SPSS (ver. 17.0). Descriptive statistics were computed to describe the data set and distribution of each variable. Any outliers were investigated and examined closely. A preliminary analysis of responses for each of the questions was conducted. The simple regression technique was used to determine the degree and direction of influence of the independent variables on the dependent variable and the statistical significance of the relationship. Moreover, regression and hierarchical regression analyses measured the degree to which independent variable (organizational culture, organizational strategy, technology, HRD) impacted to the dependent variable (organizational effectiveness) through to mediating variable (knowledge management) and moderating variable (transformational leadership).

The procedure of this regression and hierarchical analysis is presented as follows:

1. The simple regression analysis was conducted among independent variables of organizational culture, organizational strategy, technology and HRD and dependent variable of organizational effectiveness.
2. The regression analysis was also conducted to examine the mediating variable of knowledge management between independent variables of organizational culture, strategy, technology, HRD and dependent variable of organizational effectiveness.
3. The hierarchical regression analysis was conducted to examine the moderating variable of transformational leadership in the relationship between independent variable of knowledge management and dependent variable of organizational effectiveness.
4. The hypotheses were examined, each of the independent variables and their significance as related to the dependent variable; the Beta yields a positive or negative significant; R square explains the degree of prediction.

3.12 Summary

This chapter discussed the research design and the related hypotheses to the research model for further improvements in organizational effectiveness. Thus, this chapter provided detailed description of research sample, instrument, scale measures, the data procedure and data analysis. This study incorporated measurements that were adopted from previously validated instruments to form a survey instrument. A survey was conducted to R&D professionals of Mongolian Academy of Sciences (MAS). Among the 750 researchers and scientist who are working in MAS, 524 individual responses were made, which represented all 21 research institutes of MAS. Demographic, regression and hierarchical analysis was conducted on the data using SPSS (Ver-17.0).

CHAPTER 4

Key Discoveries

Abstract This chapter presents the findings of the study, presenting results from descriptive analyses, regression and hierarchical regression analyses. The chapter begins with an explanation of the sample characteristics, detailing the demographic composition of respondents from the MAS. It follows with reliability tests and validation of measurement models, demonstrating that all variables are reliable and valid, showing a good fit for each model. The study then examines the mediating effects of knowledge management and the moderating effects of transformational leadership on the relationship between various organizational factors and organizational effectiveness. The results indicate that knowledge management partially mediates the relationship between organizational culture, strategy, technology, HRD and organizational effectiveness, while transformational leadership effectively moderates the relationship between knowledge management and organizational effectiveness. The chapter concludes with a discussion of how these findings support the proposed hypotheses and their implications for enhancing organizational efficiency at MAS.

Keywords Knowledge management · Transformational leadership · Organizational effectiveness · Mediator · Moderator · Organizational culture · Organizational strategy · Technology · Human resource development

B. Dorjgotov, *Enhancing Organizational Effectiveness Through Knowledge Management and Transformational Leadership*,
https://doi.org/10.1007/978-981-97-8039-6_4

4.1 Introduction

The research model contends that organizational culture, technology, organizational strategy and HRD are preconditions required for effective knowledge management which is knowledge management mediated between organizational factors and organizational effectiveness. Effective knowledge management when moderating by transformational leadership is aimed at further improvement of organizational effectiveness. A sample frame of 750 researchers, scientists and directors in full-time employment was selected to participate in this study. From the frame of approximately 750 people working in MAS, a sample of 524 respondents (effective response rate is 69.86%) was selected for study. Six research questions were identified and analyzed using regression and hierarchical regression analysis with SPSS version-17. The five measurement models (four about mediating effects of knowledge management and one about moderating effects of transformational leadership) for analyzing the research questions were developed. The measurement models presented the theorized relationships which were tested through 15 identified hypotheses. This chapter will present the results of the relevant demographic analysis including description of sample, regression and hierarchical regression analyses including mediating effects of knowledge management, moderating effect of transformational leadership with the finding from the measurement models.

4.2 Sample Characteristics

The sample comprised 524 individual respondents who are working at the Mongolian Academy of Sciences (effective response rate is 69.86%). The Mongolian Academy of Sciences includes different kinds of scientific field environment such as social (respondents 141), engineering (respondents 24), geology/geography (respondents 124), biology/agriculture (respondents 96) and physics math/chemistry (139). Those scientific divisions (field environment) include the following research institutes and centers: Institute of Physics and Technology, Center of Astronomy and Geophysics, Institute of Informatics, Institute of Biology, Institute of Botany, Institute of Geography, Institute of Geoecology, Institute of Geology and Mineral Resources, Center of Paleontology, Institute of Chemistry and Chemical Technology, Institute of Language and Literature, Institute of History, Institute of Philosophy, Sociology and Law,

Institute of International Studies, Institute of National Development, Social Economical Research Center in Bayan-Olgee province, Institute of Archeology, International Institute for the Nomadic cultural study, Science Library, Technology transfer center and Center of Incubator. However, sample characteristics' analysis focuses on the scientific field environment which was divided into five divisions as above such as social science, engineering science, geology geography science, biology and agriculture science and physics mathematic & chemistry science. The three majorities of individual respondents were employed at the social (26.9%), physics mathematics and chemistry (26.5%) and geology geography (23.7%) sciences' division in MAS. Consequently, only a small segment of the sample was employed at the engineering (4.6%) science division in MAS. Each respondent's profile delineated along the lines of gender by scientific field environment, academic rank by scientific field environment, educational level by scientific field environment and duration of the employment by scientific field environment.

4.2.1 Gender by Scientific Field Environments

The sample consists of both males and females, characteristic of enrollment patterns in all research institutes of MAS in Mongolia. Almost similar 272 (51.9%) males and 252 (48.1%) females were presented in the sample. The social science division was represented by 84 (56.6%) males and 57 (40.4%) females, engineering science division represented 12 (50.0%) males and same as 12 (50.0%) females, geology geography science division represented by 60 (48.4%) males and 64 (51.6%) females, biology and agriculture science division represented by 41 (42.7%) males and 55 (57.3%) females, while physics mathematics and chemistry science division represented by 75 (54.0%) males and 64 (46.0%) females. Approximately, 30.6% of total male respondents from social science represent the highest percent and 25.4% of total female respondents both from physics mathematics, chemistry division and geology geography division represent the highest percent in the sample (see Table 4.1).

4.2.2 Academic Rank by Scientific Field Environment

Different countries have different systems of awarding academic ranks and degrees to scientists, scholars and faculty members of higher educational institutions. The terminology used for academic ranks and degrees in each

Table 4.1 Gender by scientific field environments

Divisions of respondent		*Gender*		*Total*
		Male	*Female*	
Social sciences	Number of respondents	84	57	141
	% within social sciences	59.6	40.4	100.0
	% within gender	30.9	22.6	26.9
	% of total	16.0	10.9	26.9
Engineering sciences	Number of respondents	12	12	24
	% within engineering sciences	50.0	50.0	100.0
	% within gender	4.4	4.8	4.6
	% of total	2.3	2.3	4.6
Geology-geography Sciences	Number of respondents	60	64	124
	% within geology-geography	48.4	51.6	100.0
	% within gender	22.1	25.4	23.7
	% of total	11.5	12.2	23.7
Biology and agriculture sciences	Number of respondents	41	55	96
	% within biology and agriculture	42.7	57.3	100.0
	% within gender	15.1	21.8	18.3
	% of total	7.8	10.5	18.3
Physics mathematics and chemistry sciences	Number of respondents	75	64	139
	% within physics mathematic and chemistry	54.0	46.0	100.0
	% within gender	27.6	25.4	26.5
	% of total	14.3	12.2	26.5
Total	Number of respondents	272	252	524
	% within gender	100.0	100.0	100.0
	% within all scientific field environments	51.9	48.1	100.0

country is determined by that country's historical development. Mongolian Academy Sciences' academic ranks conferred upon specialists with a higher education that define the extent of their graduate preparation and their scholarly qualifications and achievements in science, scholarship, technology and culture. Moreover, duration of the employment is also valued to an academic rank in MAS. Twenty two (4.2%) chief scientists, 100 (19.1%) senior scientists, 195 (37.2%) mid-level scientists, 162 (30.9%) trainee scientists, 13 (2.5%) technical staff employees and 32 (6.1%) other employees who are working in MAS were presented in the sample. The most of participates were mid-level scientists. Consequently, only small number chief scientist were participated to this study due to few number of chief scientist working in MAS. The social science division represented almost no technical staff employees participated in this division. Similarly, in engineering science division, there are no chief scientists participated in this sample.

The geology and geography sciences division was represented by 59 trainee scientists (47.6%), making it the division with the most participants. The biology and agricultural sciences division included 29 mid-level scientists (30.25%), also representing a significant number of participants. Meanwhile, the physics, mathematics, and chemistry sciences division was represented by 60 mid-level scientists (43.2%), which is again among the divisions with the most participants (see Table 4.2).

4.2.3 *Education Level by Scientific Field Environment*

The sample comprised 104 (19.8%) respondents whose last educational attainment was at a doctor degree, 233 (44.5%) with last level of educational attainment being the master degree, 149 (28.4%) with last level of educational attainment being the bachelor (undergraduate) degree, 5 (1%) with last level of educational attainment being the college certificate and 13 (2.5%) who had attained other qualifications. In addition, samples also comprised twenty (3.8%) respondents whose last scientific degree were at the post doctor (see Table 4.3).

4.2.4 *Duration of the Employment by Scientific Field Environment*

The sample comprised 181 (34.5%) respondents employed in present job for over 8 years, 62 (11.8%) employed for 5–8 years, 157 (30.0%) employed for 2–5 years and 124 (23.7%) employed for 0–2 years. The social science division was represented by 51 (36.3%) most respondents employed for over 8 years; geology geography science division was represented by 47 (37.9%) most respondents employed for 2–5 years; biology and agriculture science division was represented by 44 (45.8%) most respondents employed for over 8 years; and physics mathematic and chemistry science division represented by 43 (30.9%) most respondents employed also over 8 years (see Table 4.4).

Table 4.2 Academic rank by scientific field environments

Divisions of respondent	*Academic rank*						*Total*
	chief scientist	*Senior scientist*	*mid-level scientist*	*Trainee scientist*	*Technical staff*	*Other*	
Social sciences	7	33	66	27	N/A	8	141
	5.0%	23.4%	46.8%	19.1%	N/A	5.7%	100.0%
	31.8%	33.0%	33.8%	16.7%	N/A	25.0%	26.9%
	1.3%	6.3%	12.6%	5.2%	N/A	1.5%	26.9%
Engineering sciences	N/A	3	6	8	3	4	24
	N/A	12.5%	25.0%	33.3%	12.5%	16.7%	100.0%
	N/A	3.0%	3.1%	4.9%	23.1%	12.5%	4.6%
	N/A	0.6%	1.1%	1.5%	0.6%	0.8%	4.6%
Geology geography sciences	2	15	34	59	3	11	124
	1.6%	12.1%	27.4%	47.6%	2.4%	8.9%	100.0%
	9.1%	15.0%	17.4%	36.4%	23.1%	34.4%	23.7%
	0.4%	2.9%	6.5%	11.3%	0.6%	2.1%	23.7%
Biology and agriculture sciences	7	23	29	27	5	5	96
	7.3%	24.0%	30.2%	28.1%	5.2%	5.2%	100.0%
	31.8%	23.0%	14.9%	16.7%	38.5%	15.6%	18.3%
	1.3%	4.4%	5.5%	5.2%	1.0%	1.0%	18.3%
Physics mathematics and chemistry sciences	6	26	60	41	2	4	139
	4.3%	18.7%	43.2%	29.5%	1.4%	2.9%	100.0%
	27.3%	26.0%	30.8%	25.3%	15.4%	12.5%	26.5%
	1.1%	5.0%	11.5%	7.8%	0.4%	0.8%	26.5%
Total	22	100	195	162	13	32	524
	100.0%	100.0%	100.0%	100.0%	100.0%	100.0%	100.0%
	4.2%	19.1%	37.2%	30.9%	2.5%	6.1%	100.0%

4.3 Result from Measurement Models

The hypothesized structure model divided into five measurement models (four about mediating effects of knowledge management and one about moderating effects of transformational leadership) was developed for analyzing the research questions and presented the theorized relationships which were tested through 16 identified hypotheses. The following steps test the relationship between the organizational culture, strategy, technology, HRD, knowledge management, transformational leadership and organizational effectiveness with each measurement models. First, the study tests the significant relationships between variables. Second,

Table 4.3 Education level by scientific field environments

Divisions of respondent	*Education level*						*Total*
	College certificate	*Bachelor Degree*	*Master degree*	*Doctor degree*	*Post doctor degree*	*Other*	
Social sciences	1	22	73	35	8	2	141
	0.7%	15.6%	51.8%	24.8%	5.7%	1.4%	100.0%
	20.0%	14.8%	31.3%	33.7%	40.0%	15.4%	26.9%
	0.2%	4.2%	13.9%	6.7%	1.5%	0.4%	26.9%
Engineering sciences	1	11	7	4	0	1	24
	4.2%	45.8%	29.2%	16.7%	0.0%	4.2%	100.0%
	20.0%	7.4%	3.0%	3.8%	0.0%	7.7%	4.6%
	0.2%	2.1%	1.3%	0.8%	0.0%	0.2%	4.6%
Geology-geography sciences	1	56	44	17	2	4	124
	0.8%	45.2%	35.5%	13.7%	1.6%	3.2%	100.0%
	20.0%	37.6%	18.9%	16.3%	10.0%	30.8%	23.7%
	0.2%	10.7%	8.4%	3.2%	0.4%	0.8%	23.7%
Biology and agriculture sciences	2	21	43	19	8	3	96
	2.1%	21.9%	44.8%	19.8%	8.3%	3.1%	100.0%
	40.0%	14.1%	18.5%	18.3%	40.0%	23.1%	18.3%
	0.4%	4.0%	8.2%	3.6%	1.5%	0.6%	18.3%
Physics mathematics and chemistry sciences	0	39	66	29	2	3	139
	0.0%	28.1%	47.5%	20.9%	1.4%	2.2%	100.0%
	0.0%	26.2%	28.3%	27.9%	10.0%	23.1%	26.5%
	0.0%	7.4%	12.6%	5.5%	0.4%	0.6%	26.5%
Total	5	149	233	104	20	13	524
	1.0%	28.4%	44.5%	19.8%	3.8%	2.5%	100.0%
	100.0%	100.0%	100.0%	100.0%	100.0%	100.0%	100.0%
	1.0%	28.4%	44.5%	19.8%	3.8%	2.5%	100.0%

it examines the mediating effect of knowledge management and the moderating effect of transformational leadership, using regression and hierarchical regression analyses for each measurement model.

Gefen et al. (2000) suggested that the reliability of a variable is considered good when the composite reliability estimate exceeds 0.70. In this study, reliability was assessed by examining the reliability and validity of each variable through an evaluation of related items. The results showed that each questionnaire variable had relatively high coefficient alphas, all above 0.89 (see Table 4.5).

Table 4.4 Duration of the employment by scientific field environment

Divisions of respondent	*Duration of the employment*				*Total*
	0–2 years	*2–5 years*	*5–8 years*	*over 8 years*	
Social sciences	33	36	21	51	141
	23.4%	25.5%	14.9%	36.2%	100.0%
	26.6%	22.9%	33.9%	28.2%	26.9%
	6.3%	6.9%	4.0%	9.7%	26.9%
Engineering sciences	9	6	4	5	24
	37.5%	25.0%	16.7%	20.8%	100.0%
	7.3%	3.8%	6.5%	2.8%	4.6%
	1.7%	1.1%	0.8%	1.0%	4.6%
Geology-geography sciences	30	47	9	38	124
	24.2%	37.9%	7.3%	30.6%	100.0%
	24.2%	29.9%	14.5%	21.0%	23.7%
	5.7%	9.0%	1.7%	7.3%	23.7%
	17	28	7	44	96
	17.7%	29.2%	7.3%	45.8%	100.0%
Biology and agriculture sciences	13.7%	17.8%	11.3%	24.3%	18.3%
	3.2%	5.3%	1.3%	8.4%	18.3%
	35	40	21	43	139
	25.2%	28.8%	15.1%	30.9%	100.0%
Physics mathematics and chemistry sciences	28.2%	25.5%	33.9%	23.8%	26.5%
	6.7%	7.6%	4.0%	8.2%	26.5%
	124	157	62	181	524
	23.7%	30.0%	11.8%	34.5%	100.0%
Total	124	157	62	181	524
	23.7%	30.0%	11.8%	34.5%	100.0%
	100.0%	100.0%	100.0%	100.0%	100.0%
	23.7%	30.0%	11.8%	34.5%	100.0%

4.3.1 *Mediating Effect of Knowledge Management*

The first measurement model examined the impacts among organizational culture, knowledge management and organizational effectiveness. In terms of reliability, Cronbach's α for organizational culture was 0.941, for knowledge management 0.899 and for organizational effectiveness 0.897, all indicating reliable measures. Figure 4.1 presents the relationship between organizational culture, knowledge management and organizational effectiveness. The results of regression analysis show that

Table 4.5 Reliability for variables

Variables	*Total sample* (N = *524)* α *(no. of items)*
Mediating effects of knowledge management	
Organizational culture	0.941 (12 items)
Organizational strategy	0.926 (7 items)
Technology	0.936 (8 items)
Human resource development	0.930 (8 items)
Knowledge management	0.899 (8 items)
Moderating effects of transformational leadership	
Transformational leadership	0.949 (10 items)
Knowledge management	0.899 (8 items)
Organizational effectiveness	0.897 (8 items)

organizational culture ($\beta = 0.746$, $p < 0.001$) and knowledge management ($\beta = 0.737$, $p < 0.001$) are significant and positively related to organizational effectiveness. Moreover, organizational culture ($\beta = 0.808$, $p < 0.001$) has a significant influence on knowledge management (See Table 4.6). Therefore, H1, H2 and H13 hypotheses are supported.

In addition, the study follows Baron and Kenny (1986, p. 1177) and Krull and MacKinnon's (1999, 2001) suggestions to examine the mediating effects in four terms analysis: (1) the independent variable must affect the mediator; (2) second, the independent variable must be shown to affect the dependent variable; (3) the mediator must affect the dependent variable; and (4) If these conditions all hold in the predicted direction, then the effect of the independent variable and dependent variable must be less. The perfect mediation holds if the independent variable

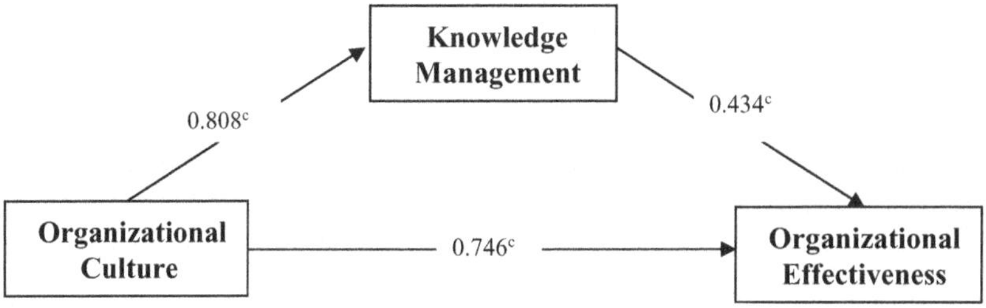

Fig. 4.1 Measurement model 1: mediating effect of knowledge management between organizational culture and organizational effectiveness ($c = p < 0.001$)

Table 4.6 Regression analysis among variables

Variables	β	R^2	F	*Sig.*
Organizational culture to knowledge management	0.808^c	0.654	984.698	0.000
Organizational culture to organizational effectiveness	0.746^c	0.557	656.670	0.000
Organizational strategy to knowledge management	0.779^c	0.607	801.600	0.000
Organizational strategy to organizational effectiveness	0.739^c	0.546	624.906	0.000
Technology to knowledge management	0.786^c	0.618	844.813	0.000
Technology to organizational effectiveness	0.736^c	0.542	617.757	0.000
HRD to knowledge management	0.728^c	0.531	588.701	0.000
HRD to organizational effectiveness	0.646^c	0.417	373.114	0.000
Knowledge management to organizational effectiveness	0.737^c	0.544	622.105	0.000

$^c p < 0.001$

has no effect to the dependent variable when the mediator is controlled. As shown in Table 4.7, the study follows Baron and Kenny's (1986) suggestions to enact the mediation test. To test hypotheses three (H3), a regression analysis needs to examine whether knowledge management has mediation effect between organizational culture and organizational effectiveness. First, the study let organizational culture as independent variable and knowledge management as mediator variable. The results show that organizational culture is significant and positively affects to knowledge management ($\beta = 0.808$, $p < 0.001$). Second, organizational culture and knowledge management are the independent variables, and organizational effectiveness is the dependent variable. The results indicate that organizational culture is significant and positively affects to organizational effectiveness ($\beta = 0.746$, $p < 0.001$). Third, knowledge management is significant and positively accounts for organizational effectiveness ($\beta = 0.737$, $p < 0.001$). Finally, organizational culture and knowledge management regressed with organizational effectiveness ($\beta = 0.434$, $p < 0.001$; $\beta = 0.387$, $p < 0.001$).

Table 4.7 Mediation test of knowledge management between organizational culture and organizational effectiveness

Variables	*Model 1*	*Model 2*		*Model 3*
	KM	*OE*	*OE*	*OE*
OC	0.808[c] (0.000)	0.746[c] (0.000)		0.434[c] (0.000)
KM			0.737[c] (0.000)	0.387[c] (0.000)
R^2	0.654	0.557	0.544	0.609
Adj R^2	0.653	0.556	0.543	0.607
F	984.698	656.67	622.105	405.637

Note OC: Organizational culture, KM: Knowledge management, OE: Organizational effectiveness
[a]$p < 0.05$, [b]$p < 0.01$, [c]$p < 0.001$

The result indicated that β value of organizational culture is reduced from 0.746 to 0.434, and both organizational culture and knowledge management are significantly related to organizational effectiveness. Therefore, hypothesis three (H3) is supported. Knowledge management provides a partial mediation effect between organizational culture and organizational effectiveness (see Table 4.7).

The second measurement model examined the impacts among HRD, knowledge management and organizational effectiveness. In terms of reliability, Cronbach's α for HRD was 0.930 indicating reliable measures. Figure 4.2 presents the relationship between HRD, knowledge management and organizational effectiveness. The results of regression analysis shows that human resource development ($\beta = 0.646$, $p < 0.001$) and knowledge management ($\beta = 0.737$, $p < 0.001$) are significant and positively related to organizational effectiveness. Moreover, HRD ($\beta = 0.728$, $p < 0.001$) have significantly influence on knowledge management (see Table 4.6). Therefore, H10, H11 and H13 hypotheses are supported.

In addition, test hypothesis twelve (H12) analyzes whether knowledge management has mediation effect between HRD and organizational effectiveness. Firstly, the study let HRD be the independent variable and knowledge management as the mediator variable. The results show that HRD is positively affected to knowledge management ($\beta = 0.728$, $p < 0.001$). Second, the study tests whether HRD affects organizational effectiveness and knowledge management affects organizational effectiveness. The results signify that HRD is positively affected to organizational

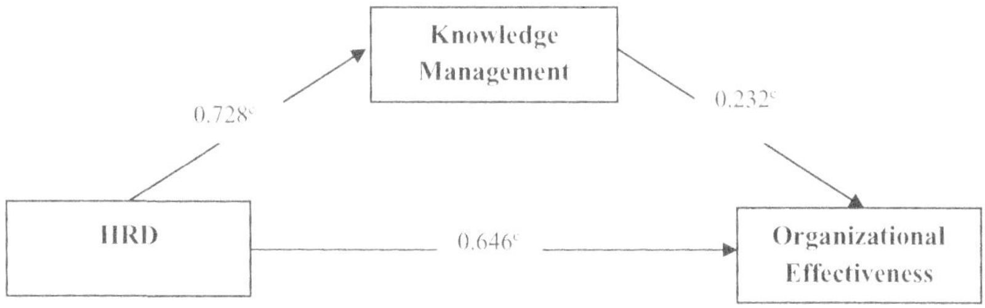

Fig. 4.2 Measurement model 2: mediating effect of knowledge management between HRD and organizational effectiveness ($c = p < 0.001$)

effectiveness ($\beta = 0.646$, $p < 0.001$). Moreover, knowledge management is significantly and positively accounted for organizational effectiveness ($\beta = 0.737$, $p < 0.001$). Third, HRD and knowledge management regressed with organizational effectiveness. The results demonstrate that HRD and knowledge management are positively affected to organizational effectiveness ($\beta = 0.232$, $p < 0.001$; $\beta = 0.569$, $p < 0.001$), and β value of the regression decreases from 0.646 to 0.232. Thus, H12 is supported and we could say that knowledge management is partial mediated in the relationship between HRD and organizational effectiveness (see Table 4.8).

The third measurement model examined the impacts among organizational strategy, knowledge management and organizational effectiveness. In terms of reliability, Cronbach's α for organizational strategy was 0.926 indicating reliable measures. Figure 4.3 presents the relationship between organizational strategy, knowledge management and organizational effectiveness. The results of regression analysis show that organizational strategy ($\beta = 0.739$, $p < 0.001$) and knowledge management ($\beta = 0.737$, $p < 0.001$) are positive and significantly related to organizational effectiveness. Moreover, organizational strategy ($\beta = 0.779$, $p < 0.001$) has a significant influence on knowledge management (see Table 4.6). Therefore, H4, H5 and H13 hypotheses are supported.

In addition, test hypothesis six (H6) analyzes whether knowledge management has a mediation effect between organizational strategy and organizational effectiveness. The study shows organizational strategy as

Table 4.8 Mediation test of knowledge management between HRD and organizational effectiveness

Variables	*Model 1*	*Model 2*		*Model 3*
	KM	*OE*	*OE*	*OE*
HRD	0.728^c (0.000)	0.646^c (0.000)		0.232^c (0.000)
KM			0.737^c (0.000)	0.569^c (0.000)
R^2	0.531	0.417	0.544	0.569
Adj R^2	0.53	0.416	0.543	0.568
F	588.701	373.114	622.105	343.609

Note HRD-Human resource development, KM-Knowledge management, OE-Organizational effectiveness
$^a p < 0.05$, $^b p < 0.01$, $^c p < 0.001$

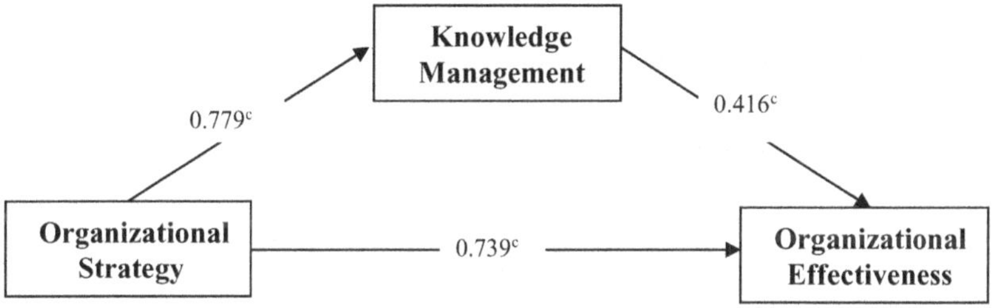

Fig. 4.3 Measurement model 3: mediating effect of knowledge management between organizational strategy and organizational effectiveness (*$c = p < 0.001$*)

an independent variable and knowledge management as a mediator variable. The results show that organizational strategy is significantly and positively affected to knowledge management ($\beta = 0.779$, $p < 0.001$). Second, organizational strategy and knowledge management are the independent variables, and organizational effectiveness is the dependent variable. The results indicate that organizational strategy is significantly and positively affected to organizational effectiveness ($\beta = 0.739$, $p < 0.001$). Moreover, knowledge management is significantly and positively accounted for organizational effectiveness ($\beta = 0.737$, $p < 0.001$). Third, organizational strategy and knowledge management regressed with organizational effectiveness ($\beta = 0.416$, $p < 0.001$; $\beta = 0.387$, $p < 0.001$).

The result indicated that β value of organizational strategy is reduced from 0.739 to 0.416, and both organizational strategy and knowledge management are significantly related to organizational effectiveness. Therefore, hypothesis six (H6) is supported. Knowledge management provides a partial mediation effect between organizational strategy and organizational effectiveness (see Table 4.9).

The fourth measurement model examined the impacts among technology, knowledge management and organizational effectiveness. In terms of reliability, Cronbach's α for technology was 0.936 indicating reliable measures. Figure 4.4 presents the relationship between technology, knowledge management and organizational effectiveness.

Table 4.9 Mediation test of knowledge management between organizational strategy and organizational effectiveness

Variables	*Model 1*	*Model 2*		*Model 3*
	KM	*OE*	*OE*	*OE*
OS	0.779^{c} (0.000)	0.739^{c} (0.000)		0.416^{c} (0.000)
KM			0.737^{c} (0.000)	0.387^{c} (0.000)
R^2	0.607	0.546	0.544	0.614
Adj R^2	0.606	0.545	0.543	0.612
F	801.6	624.906	622.105	411.923

Note OS Organizational strategy, KM Knowledge management, OE Organizational effectiveness
$^{a}p < 0.05$, $^{b}p < 0.01$, $^{c}p < 0.001$

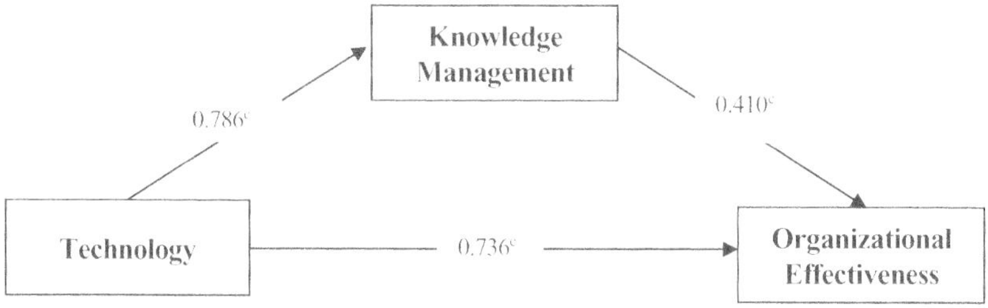

Fig. 4.4 Measurement model 4: mediating effect of knowledge management between technology and organizational effectiveness ($c = p < 0.001$)

The results of regression analysis show that technology ($\beta = 0.736$, $p < 0.001$) and knowledge management ($\beta = 0.737$, $p < 0.001$) are positive and significantly related to organizational effectiveness. Moreover, technology ($\beta = 0.786$, $p < 0.001$) has a significant influence on knowledge management (see Table 4.6). Therefore, H7, H8 and H13 hypotheses are supported.

In addition, test hypothesis nine (H9) analyzes whether knowledge management has mediation effect between technology and organizational effectiveness. At first, the study let technology to the independent variable and knowledge management be the mediator variable. The results show that technology is positively affected to knowledge management ($\beta = 0.786$, $p < 0.001$). Second, the study tests whether technology affects organizational effectiveness and knowledge management affects organizational effectiveness. The result shows that technology is positively affected to organizational effectiveness ($\beta = 0.736$, $p < 0.001$). Moreover, we already supported that knowledge management is significant and positively accounted to organizational effectiveness ($\beta = 0.737$, $p < 0.001$). Thirdly, technology and knowledge management regressed with organizational effectiveness. The results demonstrate that technology and knowledge management are positively affected to organizational effectiveness ($\beta = 0.410$, $p < 0.001$; $\beta = 0.415$, $p < 0.001$), and β value of the regression decreases from 0.736 to 0.410. Thus, H9 is supported and we also can say that knowledge management is a partial mediator between the relationship of technology and organizational effectiveness (see Table 4.10).

4.3.2 Moderating Effect of Transformational Leadership

The study also applies hierarchical regression analysis to test the research hypothesis which is focusing on the moderating effects of transformational leadership in the relationship between knowledge management and organizational effectiveness (see Fig. 4.5). As shown in Model 1, the result discloses that knowledge management ($\beta = 0.737$, $p < 0.001$) positively and significantly affected organizational effectiveness (see Table 4.11). H13 is supported. Model 2 shows that transformational leadership ($\beta = 0.715$, $p < 0.001$) positively and significantly affects organizational effectiveness. Therefore, H14 is supported.

As shown in Table 4.11, the study examines the moderating effect of transformational leadership using hierarchical regression analysis. The

Table 4.10 Mediation test of knowledge management between technology and organizational effectiveness

Variables	*Model 1*	*Model 2*		*Model 3*
	KM	*OE*	*OE*	*OE*
TE	0.786[c] (0.000)	0.736[c] (0.000)		0.410[c] (0.000)
KM			0.737[c] (0.000)	0.415[c] (0.000)
R^2	0.618	0.542	0.544	0.608
Adj R^2	0.617	0.541	0.543	0.606
F	844.813	617.757	622.105	403.812

Note TE: Technology, KM: Knowledge management, OE: Organizational effectiveness
[a]$p < 0.05$, [b]$p < 0.01$, [c]$p < 0.001$

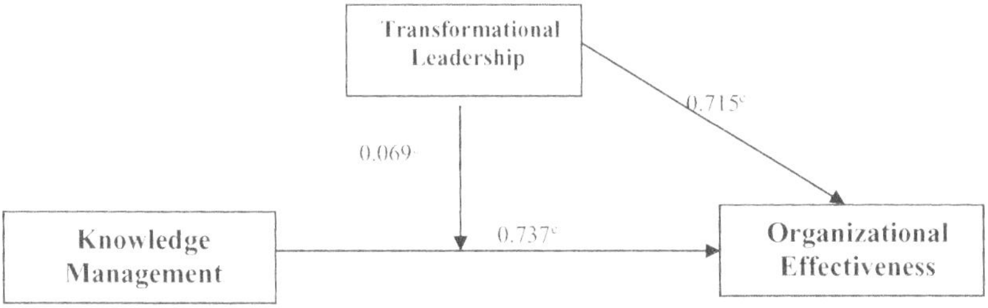

Fig. 4.5 Measurement model 5: moderating effects of transformational leadership ($a = p < 0.05$; $c = p < 0.001$)

result in Model 3 shows that both independent variables (knowledge management, $\beta = 0.459$, $p < 0.001$) and moderating variables (transformational leadership, $\beta = 0.367$, $p < 0.001$) are significantly affected to dependent variable (organizational effectiveness), respectively. In addition, the results in Model 4 reveal, the interaction effect ($R^2 = 0.604$, $\beta = 0.069$, $p < 0.05$) of knowledge management and transformational leadership is also significant to organizational effectiveness. Therefore, all hypotheses are supported.

In order to understand more about the moderating effect of transformational leadership (TL), we plotted the results using the same method shown in Aiken and West (1991). In the graph presented in Fig. 4.6, we show the effects of TL on organizational effectiveness for two levels

Table 4.11 Moderating test of transformational leadership among knowledge management and organizational effectiveness

	Model 1 *OE*	*Model 2* *OE*	*Model 3* *OE*	*Model 4* *OE*
Independent variable				
KM	0.737[c]		0.459[c]	0.477[c]
Moderating variables				
TL		0.715[c]	0.367[c]	0.394[c]
Interaction variable				
KM*TL				0.069[a]
N	524	524	524	524
Max VIF	1.000	1.000	2.353	2.588
F-value	622.105[c]	545.418[c]	391.323[c]	263.628[c]
R^2	0.544	0.511	0.601	0.604
Adj. R^2	0.543	0.511	0.599	0.601

Note OE: Organizational effectiveness; KM: Knowledge management; TL: Transformational leadership.
[a]$p < 0.05$; [b]$p < 0.01$; [c]$p < 0.001$

of TL, low and high (minus one standard deviation from the mean and plus one standard deviation from the mean, respectively). As can be seen in the reinforcement interaction effect in Fig. 4.5, the highest level of organizational effectiveness is achieved when both transformational leadership and knowledge management are high (lower scale means higher effectiveness).

4.4 Results Relating Research Questions and Hypotheses

Each research question was related to set of hypotheses and regression analysis was applied to the related hypotheses. Questions 1, 2, 3 and 4 were addressed via structural model with mediating effect of knowledge management (Figs. 4.1, 4.2, 4.3 and 4.4); while questions 5 and 6 were addressed with model with moderating effects of transformational leadership (Fig. 4.5). The research questions and related hypotheses were examined through the path (β) coefficient, and p-value.

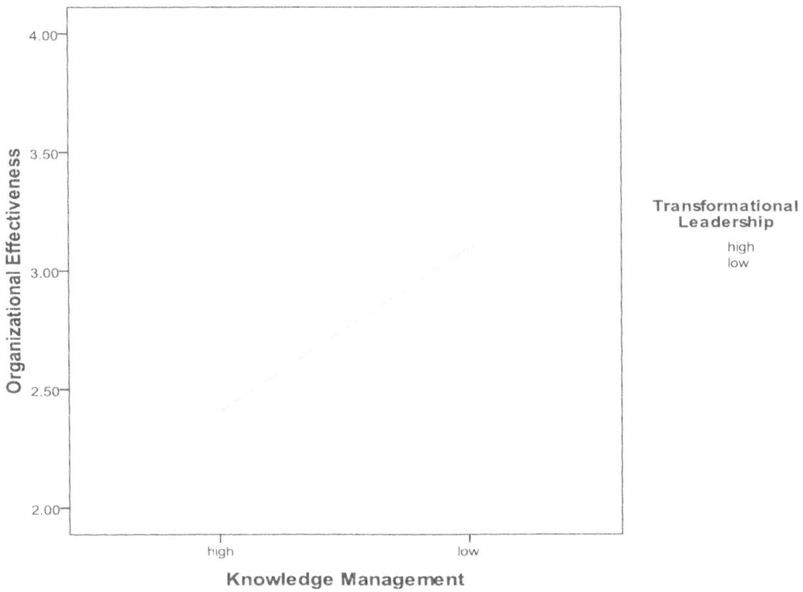

Fig. 4.6 Reinforcement interaction effects of transformational leadership, knowledge management and organizational effectiveness

Research Question 1: What are the contributions of organizational culture, organizational strategy, technology and human resource development on organizational effectiveness?

Hypothesis 2: Organizational culture (adaptability, consistency, mission and involvement) is positively and significantly affected to its organizational effectiveness.

Hypothesis 5: Organizational strategy(exploration, institutional entrepreneurship, combination and exploitation) is positively and significantly affected to organizational effectiveness.

Hypothesis 8: Technology (artifact technology, collaboration technology, distributed learning technology, knowledge mapping technology and knowledge transfer technology) is positively and significantly affected to its organizational effectiveness.

Hypothesis 11: Humanresource development (training & development, decision-making involvement, support for personal initiative and goal of communication) is positively and significantly affected to its organizational effectiveness.

Organizational culture ($\beta = 0.746$, $p < 0.001$), organizational strategy ($\beta = 0.739$, $p < 0.001$), technology ($\beta = 0.736$, $p < 0.001$) and human resource development ($\beta = 0.646$, $p < 0.001$) are positively and significantly related to organizational effectiveness. Therefore, the Research hypotheses 2, 5, 8 and 11 were supported.

Research Question 2: What are the impacts of organizational culture, organizational strategy, technology and human resource development on knowledge management?

Hypothesis 1: Organizational culture (adaptability, consistency, mission and involvement) is positively and significantly affected to its knowledge Management.
Hypothesis 4: Organizational strategy (exploration, institutional entrepreneurship, combination and exploitation) is positively and significantly affected to its knowledge Management.
Hypothesis 7: Technology (artifact technology, collaboration technology, distributed learning technology, knowledge mapping technology and knowledge transfer technology) is positively and significantly affected to its knowledge management.
Hypothesis 10: Human resource development (training & development, decision-making involvement, support for personal initiative and goal of communication) is positively and significantly affected to its knowledge management.

Organizational culture ($\beta = 0.808$, $p < 0.001$), organizational strategy ($\beta = 0.779$, $p < 0.001$), technology ($\beta = 0.786$, $p < 0.001$) and HRD ($\beta = 0.728$, $p < 0.001$) have significantly influence on knowledge management. Therefore, research hypotheses 1, 4, 7 and 10 were supported.

Research Question 3: What is the impact of knowledge management on organizational effectiveness?

Hypothesis 13: Knowledge management (knowledge creation, knowledge sharing, knowledge utilization and knowledge protection) is positively and significantly affected to its organizational effectiveness.

The knowledge management ($\beta = 0.737$, $p < 0.001$) is positively and significantly related to organizational effectiveness. It is a significant component of organizational effectiveness. So, the research hypothesis 13 was supported.

Research Question 4: How do knowledge management affecting in the relationship between organizational factors (organizational culture, organizational strategy, technology, HRD) and organizational effectiveness?

> *Hypothesis 3*: Knowledge management is a mediator between organizational culture and organizational effectiveness.
> *Hypothesis 6*: Knowledge management is a mediator between organizational strategy and organizational effectiveness.
> *Hypothesis 9*: Knowledge management is a mediator between technology and organizational effectiveness.
> *Hypothesis 12*: Knowledge management is a mediator between human resource development and organizational effectiveness.

The research result indicated that β value of organizational culture is reduced from 0.746 to 0.434, and both organizational culture and knowledge management are significantly related to organizational effectiveness. Moreover, organizational strategy is reduced from 0.739 to 0.416, and both organizational strategy and knowledge management are also significantly related to organizational effectiveness. Therefore, the research hypotheses 3 and 6 are supported. In addition, the research results also demonstrate that technology and knowledge management are positively affected to organizational effectiveness, and β value of the regression decreases from 0.736 to 0.410. Moreover, HRD and knowledge management are positively affected to organizational effectiveness, and β value of the regression decreases from 0.646 to 0.232. Thus, research hypotheses 9 and 12 were supported and knowledge management is a partial mediator between above variables (see Tables 4.7, 4.8, 4.9, 4.10).

Research Question 5: What is the impact of transformational leadership on organizational effectiveness?

> *Hypothesis 14*: Transformational leadership (idealized attributes, idealized influence, inspirational motivation, intellectual stimulation

and individualized consideration) positively affected to its organizational effectiveness.

Research results also reveal that transformational leadership ($\beta = 0.715$, $p < 0.001$) is positive and significantly affected to organizational effectiveness. Therefore, the research hypothesis 14 was supported (see Table 4.11).

Research Questions 6: How does transformational leadership affect both knowledge management and organizational effectiveness?

Hypothesis 15: Transformational leadership is a moderator between knowledge management and organizational effectiveness

The research results reveal that the interaction effect (0.069, $p < 0.05$) of knowledge management and transformational leadership is also significant to organizational effectiveness (see Table 4.11). Therefore, the research hypothesis 15 was supported.

4.5 Summary

This chapter reported on the results of the descriptive (relevant demographic), regression and hierarchical regression analyses. First, the chapter was explaining the sample characteristics. Second, the reliability test and valid measures was provided in the measurement models. The study finding shows that all variables are reliable and valid and have a good fits for each variable. Third, the study examined the mediating effects of knowledge management and moderating effects of transformational leadership using different variables of measurement models. The results of measurement models indicate that knowledge management is a partial mediator between organizational factors (culture, HRD, technology, strategy) and organizational effectiveness and transformational leadership is an effective moderator in the relationship between knowledge management and organizational effectiveness. Finally, all corresponding research hypotheses were supported.

CHAPTER 5

Conclusions and Strategic Recommendations

Abstract This chapter presents the key findings and conclusions of the research, focusing on how organizational factors such as culture, HRD, technology and strategy influence organizational effectiveness. It examines the effects of knowledge management and transformational leadership on organizational effectiveness and other factors in detail. The chapter provides statistical analyses demonstrating the direct and indirect effects of these variables. Furthermore, it offers general results and recommendations derived from the study, specifically aimed at R&D specialists and managers. The findings highlight practical implications for enhancing organizational efficiency through transformational leadership and knowledge management practices.

Keywords Knowledge management · Transformational leadership · Organizational effectiveness · Mediator · Moderator · Organizational culture · Organizational strategy · Technology · Human resource development

B. Dorjgotov, *Enhancing Organizational Effectiveness Through Knowledge Management and Transformational Leadership*, https://doi.org/10.1007/978-981-97-8039-6_5

5.1 Summary

The main purpose of this study was (1) to examine the relationship between organizational factors (culture, HRD, technology, strategy) and organizational effectiveness by focusing on mediating effects of knowledge management and (2) to examine moderating effects of transformational leadership both on knowledge management and organizational effectiveness in an R&D organization. A survey was conducted with R&D professionals and their managers' perceptions of organizational culture, HRD, technology, strategy, knowledge management, leadership and organizational effectiveness. A survey instrument was developed by adapting measures used in previous studies that assessed all variables (constructs). A sample of 21 research organization at the five scientific field environments' (divisions) was selected—social science (26.9%), physic mathematics & chemistry science (26.5%), geology & geography science (23.7%), biology & agriculture science (18.3%) and engineering science (4.6%) divisions' in Mongolian Academy of Sciences. Among the 750 R&D professionals contacted, 524 responses were received, a response rate of 69.89%. Regression, hierarchical regression analysis using SPSS-17 version was used to analyze the data. The study also included the descriptive insights for sampling characteristics.

The main results of this study summarize as follows: The first, the results of study showed that organizational culture, HRD, technology and organizational strategy have significantly impacted on knowledge management. Among the organizational factors, organizational culture had the largest positive effect on knowledge management ($\beta = 0.808$, $p < 0.001$). However, other factors also was shown to have a highest positive impact on knowledge management, followed by technology significantly and positive impacted on knowledge management ($\beta = 0.786$, $p < 0.001$), organizational strategy positive impacted on knowledge management ($\beta = 0.779$, $p < 0.001$) and HRD was shown to have significantly and positive impacted on knowledge management ($\beta = 0.728$, $p < 0.001$).

Secondly, the study also examined the direct effects between organizational factors (culture, HRD, technology, strategy) and organizational effectiveness. The result of study found that all organizational factors (organizational culture, HRD, technology and organizational strategy) were shown to have a positive direct impact on organizational effectiveness, followed by organizational culture ($\beta = 0.746$, $p < 0.001$), human resource development ($\beta = 0.646$, $p < 0.001$), organizational strategy (β

= 0.739, $p < 0.001$) and technology ($\beta = 0.736$, $p < 0.001$) have significantly impacted on organizational effectiveness. In addition, the study found that knowledge management has been significantly associated with organizational effectiveness ($\beta = 0.737$, $p < 0.001$).

Thirdly, the study follows Baron and Kenny's (1986) suggestions to enact the mediation test of knowledge management between organizational factors (organizational culture, HRD, technology and organizational strategy) and organizational effectiveness. So, the results of study indicated that organizational culture did have a direct influence on organizational effectiveness ($\beta = 0.746$, $p < 0.001$). In another way, organizational culture also did have an indirect effect on organizational effectiveness through knowledge management ($\beta = 0.434$, $p < 0.001$). The mediation test indicated that β value of organizational culture is reduced from 0.746 to 0.434. This means knowledge management has a partial mediator between organizational culture and organizational effectiveness. In addition, HRD was indicated a direct effect on both knowledge management ($\beta = 0.728$, $p < 0.001$) and organizational effectiveness ($\beta = 0.646$, $p < 0.001$). Moreover, HRD also has an indirect influence on organizational effectiveness which was mediated by knowledge management ($\beta = 0.232$, $p < 0.001$). It means, knowledge management is a partial mediator between HRD and organizational effectiveness due to HRD of β value decreases from 0.646 to 0.232.

Organizational strategy was found to have a direct effect on both knowledge management ($\beta = 0.779$, $p < 0.001$) and organizational effectiveness ($\beta = 0.739$, $p < 0.001$). We defined that knowledge management as being significantly related to organizational effectiveness. Moreover, organizational strategy also did have an indirect effect on organizational effectiveness through knowledge management ($\beta = 0.416$, $p < 0.001$). The result also indicated that β value of organizational strategy is reduced from 0.739 to 0.416. Therefore, knowledge management is a partial mediator between organizational strategy and organizational effectiveness. Furthermore, the study showed that technology did have a direct and positive impact on knowledge management ($\beta = 0.786$, $p < 0.001$) and organizational effectiveness ($\beta = 0.736$, $p < 0.001$). However, technology also has an indirect effect on organizational effectiveness through knowledge management and the β value of technology decreased from 0.736 to 0.410. It means knowledge management is a partial mediator between technology and organizational effectiveness.

Finally, the study was to examine the moderating effects of transformational leadership on both knowledge management and organizational effectiveness. The study identified that knowledge management has a direct influence on organizational effectiveness ($\beta = 0.737$, $p < 0.001$). The findings also indicated transformational leadership did have a positive influence on organizational effectiveness ($\beta = 0.715$, $p < 0.001$). Then, the study uses hierarchical regression analysis to examine the moderating effect of transformational leadership. The results reveal that both independent variable (knowledge management, $\beta = 0.459$, $p < 0.001$) and moderating variables (transformational leadership, $\beta = 0.367$, $p < 0.001$) are significantly affected to dependent variable (organizational effectiveness) respectively. In addition, the interaction effects ($R^2 = 0.604$, $\beta = 0.069$, $p < 0.05$) of knowledge management and transformational leadership are significantly affected on organizational effectiveness. Therefore, transformational leadership is an effective moderator between knowledge management and organizational effectiveness. Since we plotted the results using the same method shown in Aiken and West (1991), we can analyze the findings accordingly. The results show that transformational leadership and knowledge management have a reinforcement interaction effect on organizational effectiveness, and they do so interactively. Therefore, transformational leadership is important for improving organizational effectiveness, especially interacting with knowledge management in organizational level.

5.2 Discussion

The study results are discussed in the following sections. The sections are organized by the research questions and related hypotheses.

What Are the Contributions of Organizational Culture, Organizational Strategy, Technology and Human Resource Development on Organizational Effectiveness?

The study result supported that organizational culture, HRD, technology and organizational strategy had a direct impact on organizational effectiveness.

Basically, organizational effectiveness diagnosis involves to understanding important organizational factors and then identifying how the organizational factors relate to organizational effectiveness. Assessing organizational effectiveness provides the necessary practical understanding to devise for solving problems and improving organizational performance. Historically, organizational effectiveness is evaluated to focus on how well organizations compete, how quickly they bring products to market, their status in the community, their attractiveness to potential employees and their profitability. In other words, organizational effectiveness is the extent to which an organization is meeting its functional goals. Assessing and improving effectiveness of an organization is more elusive than it appears. Because, it is unclear whether you can decide on a single set goal or, for that matter, come to consensus about multiple set goals for an organization (Brown, 1994). Also, it is unclear where to go, and to whom to go to, to identify goals or seek consensus. However, organizational effectiveness is likely to be high when there is good alignment. Organizational culture, HRD, technology and organizational strategy are explained nearly in organizational effectiveness. Those factors are prerequisite for organizational effectiveness. The following paragraphs discuss their respective impact on organizational effectiveness.

Organizational Culture and Its Impact on Organizational Effectiveness

Organizational culture did influence organizational effectiveness directly ($\beta = 0.746$, $p < 0.001$). Many studies have focused on the direct relationship between organizational culture and organizational effectiveness (Denison, 1990; Denison & Mishra, 1995; Denison et al., 2004; Fey & Denison, 2003). The current study reached similar conclusion as previous studies that organizational culture is a key factor to organizational effectiveness and it could be a source of sustained competitive advantage for organization. However, the study showed that organizational culture's influence on organizational effectiveness decreased when a mediator (by reason of knowledge management) was considered.

Human Resource Development Its Impact on Organizational Effectiveness

Human resource development (HRD) was shown to examine positive direct effect on organizational effectiveness ($\beta = 0.646$, $p < 0.001$). As the dimensions of HRD consist of training and development of employees, decision-making involvement, personal initiative and goal of communication, the results mean the four dimensions combined facilitate organizational effectiveness. In addition, the study suggest more investment in trainings and development programs, promotion planning and other HRD activities to prove effective outcomes related to an organization's core competencies and human capital. Hence, maintaining high human resource development activities should have positive consequences on organizational effectiveness and performance. However, the study showed that HRD's influence on organizational effectiveness was degreasing when a mediator (by reason of knowledge management) was considered.

Technology Its Impact on Organizational Effectiveness

The study showed that technology did have a direct influence on organizational effectiveness ($\beta = 0.736$, $p < 0.001$). Typically, technological resources of an organization encompass all of the equipment, machinery and systems that are essential for the organization to function properly. The new method and applications of IT development facilitate (such as groupware, online databases, internet, etc.) and allow firms to deliver better quality' product and services and thus firms achieve competitive advantage and profit. It seems technologies are conceptually complex and multi-dimensional. As we known, technology exists in many forms including artifact, knowledge and process. In this study, as the constructs of technology consisted of artifact, collaboration, distributed learning, knowledge mapping and knowledge sharing technologies, the results mean that the five technology's dimensions combined facilitate organizational effectiveness. However, the study findings showed that technology's influence on organizational effectiveness decreased when a mediator (by reason of knowledge management) was considered.

Organizational Strategy Its Impact on Organizational Effectiveness

Organizational strategy did have a direct influence on organizational effectiveness ($\beta = 0.739$, $p < 0.001$). Historically, strategies are often developed at different levels with different perspectives. Defining strategy allows researchers to move beyond the abstract and normative aspects of strategy toward those different decisions which actually involve organizational goals and the allocation of resources necessary to achieve goals (Snow & Hambrick, 1980). In the present study, organizational strategy is drawn based on knowledge creation process and consists the exploration, institutional entrepreneurship, combination and exploitation. If knowledge is considered a creation process and is an important determinant of organizational performance, then knowledge creation strategies are likely to be a key area of strategic choice for the organization. Generally, the strategy is understood as the pattern or plan that integrates an organization's major goals, policies and action sequence into a cohesive whole. It is a high-level, long-term meta-plan that determines the ultimate success and viability of an organization. The results indicate the knowledge creation strategy's four dimensions combined facilitate organizational effectiveness. However, the study also indicated that organizational strategy influence on organizational effectiveness decreased when a mediator was considered.

What Are the Impacts of Organizational Culture, Organizational Strategy, Technology and Human Resource Development on Knowledge Management?

While present study showed that organizational culture, HRD, technology and organizational strategy had a significant and positive influence on knowledge management. The following paragraphs discuss their respective impact on knowledge management.

Organizational Culture Its Impact on Knowledge Management

The results of this study shown organizational culture had the largest positive influence on knowledge management ($\beta = 0.808$, $p < 0.001$). In this study, organizational culture was represented by four dimensions namely involvement, consistency, adaptability and mission. From the results of measurement model, these four dimensions were found to be positively correlated with each other and with the overall constructs of organizational culture. Turban and Arison (2001) has emphasized that the ability of an organization to learn, develop memory and share knowledge is dependent on its culture. The study finding also suggests that how knowledge is managed well is greatly associated with how well cultural values are translated into value to the organization. This may be due to the culture determining the basic beliefs, values and norms regarding knowledge creation, conversion, utilization and protection among organization.

HRD Its Impact on Knowledge Management

The findings showed that HRD had a positive influence on knowledge management ($\beta = 0.728$, $p < 0.001$). The theoretical literature suggested that human resource management increases productivity by increasing employees' skill and motivation (Huselid, 1995). Thus, it is clear to achieve competitive advantage, organizations need to generate specific knowledge because specific resources are unique and difficult to imitate. One way to generate firm-specific resource (knowledge) is human resource development. In addition, HRD skills and knowledge are critical to the success of knowledge management processes, whatever perspective on knowledge could be used. So, the study suggests that managers should give more attention on how to improve their employees' skills through HRD, and it might generate more firm-specific resources for organization's success in future.

Technology Its Impact on Knowledge Management

The study results shown that technology had substantially and positive influence on knowledge management ($\beta = 0.786$, $p < 0.001$). Most people have little difficulty expressing some notion of what it is for technology. For instance, technology is science plus purpose. While science is the study of laws of nature, technology is the practical application of those laws toward the achievement of some purposes. One parts of scholars' defined technology as the organization of knowledge for the achievement of practical purpose. In the twenty-first century, new technologies have become the important catalysts in changing the way business is being conducted. For instance, managing knowledge is about managing your people to use information on customers, products, processes and partners to create knowledge for organization. Becoming a knowledge-driven organization requires a new way of thinking and a new mindset that crosses all boundaries between profit and non-for-profit organizations and between different sizes of organizations (Kermally, 2002). Thus, technology had enabled many organizations to capture and manage such information. The above concepts lead that science and technology are woven throughout a larger complex of human activity which is oriented around a mix of economic, political, humanitarian and cultural means and ends. To make this happen, technology was playing a major role in the present study for knowledge management and organizational effectiveness. Thus, the appropriate technology can significantly improve the efficiency and effectiveness of knowledge management.

Organizational Strategy Its Impact on Knowledge Management

The result findings indicate that organizational strategy ($\beta = 0.779$, $p < 0.001$) had positive influence on knowledge management. In this study, we used the organizational creation strategy including the dimensions of socialization, externalization, combination and internalization. Organizational knowledge creation is "the capability of a company as a whole to create new knowledge, disseminate it throughout the organizational and embody it in products, services and systems". While the organizational creation strategy is important in explaining how new knowledge is generated or how existing knowledge can be replicated to affect certain organizational outcomes. It is clear that a particular intangible resource has become the cornerstone of sustainable competitive advantage in the knowledge based view of the organization. Several executives and managers are stressed to articulate the relationship between their firm's competitive strategy and its intellectual resources and capabilities. Perhaps, well-developed strategic models that help them to link knowledge creation processes to business strategy. However, they are not sure of the way to translate the goal of making their organizations more intellectual into a strategic action (Yang et al., 2009). Therefore, if knowledge and its creation process is so important, a determinant of organizational performance and then knowledge creation strategies are likely to be a key area of strategic choice for the organization especially in R&D settings.

What Is the Impact of Knowledge Management on Organizational Effectiveness?

Knowledge management had significant and positive impact on organizational effectiveness ($\beta = 0.737$, $p < 0.001$). It is essential results in this study and it supported to manage knowledge that is associated with organizational effectiveness. Moreover, this kind of finding corresponded to several authors (Davenport & Prusak, 1998; Gold et al., 2001; Nonaka & Takeuchi, 1995; Zheng et al., 2009). Some of their study results through knowledge creation. The insights of individuals are converted into knowledge that can be used to design new products or improve performance (Nonaka & Takeuchi, 1995) and knowledge management has been regarded as contributing to enhancing organizational effectiveness (Davenport & Prusak, 1998). The finding of this study added another piece of empirical evidence to the relationship between knowledge management and organizational effectiveness.

How Do Knowledge Management Affecting in the Relationship Between Organizational Factors (Organizational Culture, Organizational Strategy, Technology, HRD) and Organizational Effectiveness?

Importantly, findings shows that knowledge management has a mediator between organizational factors (organizational culture, HRD, technology and organizational strategy) and organizational effectiveness. The results indicated that β value of organizational culture is reduced from 0.746 to 0.434, β value of the HRD decreases from 0.646 to 0.232, β value of the technology decreases from 0.736 to 0.410 and β value of organizational strategy is reduced from 0.739 to 0.416 when mediating effects of knowledge management was considered. The findings supported that knowledge management is a partial mediator among the above variables. It means knowledge management is not only an independent effect on organizational effectiveness, but it is also a central mechanism that leverages organizational factors (organizational culture, HRD, technology and organizational strategy) to influence organizational effectiveness. Thus, the study resulted that both organizational factors (organizational culture, HRD, technology and organizational strategy) and knowledge management are significantly and simultaneously influenced on organizational effectiveness. It appears that the next research on the relationship between organizational factors (organizational culture, HRD, technology, organizational strategy) and organizational effectiveness should investigate deeper level by examining the specific mechanism through how organizational factors effectively influence organizational effectiveness through indirect interrelationship with other factors such as knowledge management. As we know, knowledge is an appreciating asset. The more it is used, the more effective its application. In a modern context, businesses have to come up with innovative structures and thinking in order to gain superior performance. Therefore, understand the importance of knowledge as a key organizational capability and use it to gain superior performance (Kermally, 2002).

What Is the Impact of Transformational Leadership on Organizational Effectiveness?

Transformational leadership played a favorable factor on organizational effectiveness and this study results in transformational leadership and had a positive impact on organizational effectiveness (β = 0.715, p <

0.001). Previous research has demonstrated that transformational leadership appears to be an effective style for use in R&D settings (Elkins & Keller, 2003; Keller et al., 1992). Crawford's (2005) recent research emphasized that transformational leaders are better suited to handle even the most technical aspects of the modern workplace than transactional or laissez-faire leaders. In order to that, this transformational leader's behaviors are likely to act that as "creativity enhancing forces"; individuals consideration "serves as a reward" for followers by providing recognition and encouragement; intellectual stimulation "enhance exploratory thinking" by providing support for innovation, autonomy and challenge; and inspirational motivation "provides encouragement into the idea generation process" by energizing followers to work toward the organization's vision (Bass & Avolio, 1995; Sosik et al., 2003).

How Does Transformational Leadership Affect the Relationship Between Knowledge Management and Organizational Effectiveness?

The examination of the results revealed that transformational leadership had an effective moderator in the relationship between knowledge management and organizational effectiveness. The results of study shows that both independent variable (knowledge management, $\beta = 0.459$, $p < 0.001$) and moderating variables (transformational leadership, $\beta = 0.367$, $p < 0.001$) are significantly affected to dependent variable (organizational effectiveness), respectively. In addition, the interaction effects ($R^2 = 0.604$, $\beta = 0.069$, $p < 0.05$) of knowledge management and transformational leadership are positively affected to organizational effectiveness. This means that the strength or direction of the relationship between the knowledge management and organizational effectiveness is significantly affected by the moderator variable of transformational leadership. This type of moderator relationship is of primary importance in organizational effectiveness and it will be future improve organizational performance. Organization can benefit greatly from considering if potential moderator variable such as organizational members characteristics and leader's behavioral components' significantly influence on organizational ability to affect organizational effectiveness. The study results also clarified to support transformational leadership and knowledge management has a reinforcement interaction effect on organizational effectiveness, and they do so interactively. Therefore, transformational leadership is important for improving organizational effectiveness, especially interacting with knowledge management in an organization. It seems transformational leadership could be encouraging creativity and change in employees and continuous facilitation of their development.

5.3 Limitation

Only one limitations of this study need to be highlighted through surveys. The study results comes out from the R&D professionals and their managers' perception of organizational culture, strategy, technology and HRD, knowledge management, transformational leadership and organizational effectiveness. Hence, the study results were generated from R&D organizations in Mongolia. Thus, the research result might not be representative to the organization of in other countries.

5.4 Implication and Recommendation

The study implication can be focused on two major themes including knowledge management and transformational leadership. The study recommendation will be a response to the last research question of "how to effectively manage R&D based organization, and lead to motivate research scientists and engineers for a successful future?"

5.4.1 Implications

The importance of this study is to contribute to management learning research by providing a conceptual model for describing and evaluating an organizational effectiveness and its relationship with knowledge management and transformational leadership. Organizational effectiveness evaluation involves understanding the importance of organizational factors and then identifying how those organizational factors effecting on organizational effectiveness. The evaluation of organizational effectiveness provides the necessary practical understanding to devise for solving problems and improving organizational performance. Based on the findings of this study, implications for improving organizational effectiveness in terms of using the two power base (knowledge management and transformational leadership) are addressed as follows:

The first, in this study, we supported that knowledge management is a partial mediator between organizational factors (culture, HRD, technology and strategy) and organizational effectiveness. It means knowledge management is not only an independent predict to organizational effectiveness, it is also a central mechanism that leverages organizational culture, HRD, technology and organizational strategy to influence on organizational effectiveness. It seems how knowledge is managed well is greatly associated with how well cultural, HRD, technology and strategy values are translated into value to the organization. Organizational culture may determine the basic beliefs, values and norms regarding knowledge creation, conversion, utilization and protection among organization or individuals. Organizations can generate specific knowledge through to human resource development of because specific resources are unique and difficult to imitate and could achieve competitive advantage. Thus, HRD increases organizational effectiveness by increasing employees' skill and motivation. The technology refers to the crucial element of the structural dimension needed to mobilize social capital for the creation of knowledge (Gold et al., 2001) and ICT enables knowledge management activities for collaborative decision support, information sharing, organizational learning and organizational memory. From another points, advanced IT applications and network systems facilitate employee knowledge sharing, employees are the main driver of knowledge and information sharing in organizations. Moreover, both endogenous and exogenous knowledge through IT applications significantly enhances dynamic capabilities and it seems organizations ought to give particular attention to KM in order to enhance dynamic capabilities and help to ensure excellence and competitiveness. The organizational knowledge creation strategies provided useful framework for employees to generate new knowledge. Thus, it seems that knowledge management effectively influence on organizational effectiveness when it is clearly alignment with organizational culture, HRD, technology and organizational strategy. Therefore, knowledge management is a critical factor for organization's success and competitiveness in an R&D organization in Mongolia. However, organization may not be equally predisposed for successful launch and maintenance of knowledge management initiatives. Therefore, a key to understanding the success and failure of knowledge management within organization is the identification and assessment of preconditions that are necessary for the effort to flourish.

Secondly, almost any empirical study investigated moderating effect of transformational leadership in the relationship between knowledge management and organizational effectiveness. Therefore, the study finding also contributes to organizational theory by exploring the moderating effects of transformational leadership. Transformational leader's behaviors are likely to act that creativity enhancing force; to serves as a reward for followers by providing recognition and encouragement; to enhance exploratory thinking by providing support for innovation, autonomy and challenge; to provide encouragement into the idea generation process by energizing followers to work toward the organization's vision. Hence, transformational leaders' behaviors create an effective and meaningful workplace for organization members and it will be future improve knowledge creation and organizational success. The study results also support that transformational leadership and knowledge management has a reinforcement interaction effect on organizational effectiveness, they do so interactively. Therefore, transformational leadership is important for improving organizational effectiveness especially interacting with knowledge management in an R&D organization. Hence, transformational leadership could be encouraging creativity and change in employees and continuous facilitation of their development.

5.4.2 *Recommendation for R&D Professional and Managers*

In the twenty-first century, knowledge and innovation have played an important role in both national and global economic development. The ability to create, disseminate and exploit knowledge is a major source of competitiveness, wealth creation and enhancement of quality of life. A nation's knowledge capabilities clearly underpin its competitive advantages and growth potential. Especially, Asian economies, such as South Korea, Taiwan and Singapore, have transformed their economies by improving the results of the accumulation of knowledge and the advanced technologies of their industries through purposeful science and technology policies. Contrary, many nations are rich in natural resources. However, they cannot develop themselves due to shortage of well-trained manpower as well as badly managed science & technology infrastructure. From this point, governments are responsible for developing the science and technological structure and the appropriate institutions and macro-economic policies to support R&D. For example, the presence of a well-developed science and technological infrastructure (encompassing the network of research organizations, the education system) as well as institutions to protect intellectual property rights provides the foundation for the development of innovation capabilities and the pursuit of scientific research and endeavors. The multifaceted R&D capabilities of a nation include indicators such as the patenting rates, number of research scientists and engineers, as well as the output of scientific publications (Koh, 2006). In order to achieve sustainable economic growth, it is urgent in Mongolia that the R&D organizations need to be establish an effective R&D management system. In addition, we should know that something is happening in the world business. This event has been developing for the last three decide and has gathered momentum during two decide. This activity has managed to influence governments, international business professionals, consultants, academics and respected writers. This event is real, it is happening now and it is not going away. It is the knowledge economy. This kind of modern economic system is increasing based on knowledge management. Why knowledge management is important for every professionals today, especially for Mongolian Academy of Sciences (MAS). The reason that knowledge management itself as the management discipline of the two decide is because it is about people. Knowledge management is unique and employees benefit from this business process. Different organizations (governmental, commercial and educational) will weigh the available criteria differently. For MAS, many units of output are intangible and subjective in nature. For instance: in pure research, the publication criterion is weighted more heavily, and in applied research, the product that has been invented or developed is the key output in MAS. Therefore, based on knowledge management, they can contribute more, they can learn more, they can understand more and they can get benefits. In addition, understanding and measuring the impacts of knowledge management are crucial in the R&D organization as well as National Science and Technology policies in Mongolia.

The result of study reveals that knowledge management can strongly influence organizational effectiveness when it is alignment with organizational culture, HRD, technology and organizational strategy. The effective knowledge management is a valuable organizational asset. Focus on knowledge management such as providing knowledge management tools, involving effective knowledge management method, to supporting knowledge management initiatives, to enlarging the knowledge base that improving its use will contribute to the organizational success. In addition, organizational culture, HRD, technology, organizational strategy are highly relating with knowledge management. Among above variables, organizational culture has the strongest positive influence on knowledge management in the study area. This implies knowledge management practices need to center on incorporating culture-building activities to foster an environment that is knowledge-friendly R&D organization of Mongolia. Contemporary management thinking is being profoundly reshaped by two new convictions: first, managing organizational knowledge effectively is essential to achieving competitive success; second, managing knowledge is now a central concern and must become a basic skill of the modern manager.

Furthermore, Organizations are now even more concerned with identifying the effective leadership styles necessary to motivate employees in uncertain conditions. The results of study supported that transformational leadership plays a significant role in enhancing several aspect of effectiveness in R&D settings its same as pervious studies' result. Importantly, transformational leaders could enhance innovation within the organization. Organization innovation is the creation of valuable and useful new product and services within in organizational context. Since most organizations engage in innovative activity as a competitive weapon, innovation through creativity is an important factor in the success and competitive advantage of organization as well as strong economy. The global trends and experiences show that today's economies are developed by utilizing intellectual capacity of society in dynamic socio-economic growth, by developing an effective education and innovation systems based on "knowledge based" environment. Leaders' use of inspirational motivation and intellectual stimulation is critical for organizational innovation (Elkins & Keller, 2003). These leaders have a vision that motivates followers, increases their willingness to perform beyond expectations and challenges them to adopt innovative approaches in their work. The findings of study should encourage R&D managers to engage in transformational leadership behaviors in order to creating new knowledge, idea of their employees and to bring success organizational innovation and that will be future to improve organizational competitive advantage.

Appendix A: Consent Form by English

Consent Form

You are invited to participate in a dissertation study on the relationship among organizational culture, strategy, technology, HRD, knowledge management, transformational leadership and organizational effectiveness.

Expected participants are R&D professionals who had/have experience working in the Mongolian Academy of Sciences.

This study was conducted by BATTOGTOKH Dorjgotov, a Ph.D candidate of Management sciences, at the Department of Business Administration, Nanhua University, Taiwan. This study has been approved by the committee members at the Nanhua University.

Background Information

The purpose of this study is to investigate the impacts among organizational culture, strategy, technology, human resource development (HRD), transformational leadership, knowledge management and organizational effectiveness.

B. Dorjgotov, *Enhancing Organizational Effectiveness Through Knowledge Management and Transformational Leadership*, https://doi.org/10.1007/978-981-97-8039-6

Procedures

The survey will ask you to identify the characteristics of your organization's culture, strategy, technology, HRD, knowledge management, leadership behaviors and organizational effectiveness, based on your observation.

It takes appropriately 20 minutes to complete survey.

Risks and Benefits of Being in the Study

This study will give you an opportunity to view your organization from your multiple perspectives of culture, strategy, technology and HRD. It also may provide new ideas as to how to improving organizational effectiveness through to knowledge management and transformational leadership from different angles. The study might cause a slight dissatisfaction if you come across some unsatisfactory aspects of your organization.

Confidentiality

The records of this study will be kept private. In any report the researcher might publish, the researcher will not include any information that will make it possible to identify you or your organization. Only the researcher and researcher's advisors will have access to the data.

Voluntary Nature of the Study

Your decision to participate or not will not affect your current or future relations with the Mongolian Academy of Science and your organization. If you decide to participate, you are free to withdraw at any time without affecting those relationships.

Contact and Questions

You may contact the researcher Battogtokh, D at dbat_ig@yahoo.com, or by phone at 976-99716151. The researcher's advisors are Dr. Hsinkuang Chi and Dr. Chun-Hsiung Lan. You may contuct Dr. Hsinkuang Chi at kuangchi@ms10.hinet.net or by phone at 886-5-2721001 Ext.50207. You may contact Dr. Chun-Hsiung Lan at chlan@mail.nhu.edu.tw or by phone at 886-5-2721001 ext 56519.

If you have any questions or concerns regarding the study and would like to talk to someone other than the researcher and the advisors, contact coordinator (Ms. Shih) at msshih@mail.nhu.edu.tw or by phone at +886-5-2721001 ext 2071 2081, Department of Business Administration, Nanhua University, No. 32, Jhong Valley, Dalin Township, Chiayi County 622, Taiwan (R.O.C.)

You can copy and keep this page for your record

If you agree to participate in this study, please sign here to indicate you have read to consent form and return this page together with your completed questionnaire.

_______________________________________ (Your signature)

Appendix B: Survey Questionnaire by English

Survey Questionnaire

Thank you very much for participating in this survey! Your input is very valuable. Please answer the following questions regarding your organization based on your current perceptions.

You will be asked to rate how each statement describes your organization. Answers can range from strongly agree (1), agree (2), slightly agree (3), neither agree or nor disagree (4), slightly disagree (5), disagree (6) and to strongly disagree (7). It will take approximately 20 minutes to complete the questionnaire.

		Strongly agree	*Agree*	*Slightly agree*	*Neither agree or nor disagree*	*Slightly disagree*	*Disagree*	*Strongly disagree*
1	Our organization's ability to obtain more research fund is improving	1	2	3	4	5	6	7

(continued)

B. Dorjgotov, *Enhancing Organizational Effectiveness Through Knowledge Management and Transformational Leadership*,
https://doi.org/10.1007/978-981-97-8039-6

(continued)

		Strongly agree	*Agree*	*Slightly agree*	*Neither agree or nor disagree*	*Slightly disagree*	*Disagree*	*Strongly disagree*
2	Our organization has improved its ability to increase the number of reports, publication and new products	1	2	3	4	5	6	7
3	Our organization has improved its ability to increase the number of received patent	1	2	3	4	5	6	7
4	Our organization has improved its ability to quickly adapt its aim and goals to industry/market changes	1	2	3	4	5	6	7
5	Our organization has improved its ability to ensure that individual goals are consistent with organizational goals	1	2	3	4	5	6	7
6	Our organization has improved its ability to foresee risks and benefits	1	2	3	4	5	6	7
7	Our organization has improved its ability to innovate new products/services	1	2	3	4	5	6	7
8	Our organization has improved its ability to rapidly commercialize new innovations	1	2	3	4	5	6	7

(continued)

(continued)

		Strongly agree	*Agree*	*Slightly agree*	*Neither agree or nor disagree*	*Slightly disagree*	*Disagree*	*Strongly disagree*
9	Our organization acquires new knowledge from existing knowledge	1	2	3	4	5	6	7
10	Our organization generates knowledge about new product/ services within our industry	1	2	3	4	5	6	7
11	Our organization has process for transferring organizational knowledge to individuals	1	2	3	4	5	6	7
12	Our organization has a process to absorb knowledge from individuals into organization	1	2	3	4	5	6	7
13	Our organization has process to apply knowledge learned from mistakes/ experiences	1	2	3	4	5	6	7
14	Our organization has a process to improve their efficiency by using their knowledge	1	2	3	4	5	6	7
15	Our organization has a process to protect knowledge from inappropriate use inside the organization	1	2	3	4	5	6	7

(continued)

(continued)

		Strongly agree	*Agree*	*Slightly agree*	*Neither agree or nor disagree*	*Slightly disagree*	*Disagree*	*Strongly disagree*
16	Our organization has processes to protect knowledge from inappropriate use from outside the organization	1	2	3	4	5	6	7
17	Our organization's leader/manager instills pride in me for being associated with him/her	1	2	3	4	5	6	7
18	Our organization's leader/manager shows a sense of power and confidence	1	2	3	4	5	6	7
19	Our organization's leader/manager talks about our most important values and beliefs	1	2	3	4	5	6	7
20	Our organization's leader/manager specifies the importance of having a strong sense of purpose	1	2	3	4	5	6	7
21	Our organization's leader/manager talks optimistically about the future	1	2	3	4	5	6	7

(continued)

(continued)

		Strongly agree	*Agree*	*Slightly agree*	*Neither agree or nor disagree*	*Slightly disagree*	*Disagree*	*Strongly disagree*
22	Our organization's leader/manager talks enthusiastically about what needs to be accomplished	1	2	3	4	5	6	7
23	Our organization's leader/manager re-examines critical assumptions to question whether they are appropriate	1	2	3	4	5	6	7
24	Our organization's leader/manager suggests new ways to complete assignments	1	2	3	4	5	6	7
25	Our organization's leader/manager treats me as an individual rather than just as a member of a group	1	2	3	4	5	6	7
26	Our organization's leader/manager helps me to develop my ability	1	2	3	4	5	6	7

(continued)

(continued)

		Strongly agree	*Agree*	*Slightly agree*	*Neither agree or nor disagree*	*Slightly disagree*	*Disagree*	*Strongly disagree*
27	In our organization, information is widely shared so that everyone can get the information whenever he or she need	1	2	3	4	5	6	7
28	In our organization, people work like they are part of team	1	2	3	4	5	6	7
29	The capability of people in this organization is viewed as a main source of competitive advantage	1	2	3	4	5	6	7
30	If there are difficult issues or problems in our organization we solve them simply	1	2	3	4	5	6	7
31	Our organization implements projects simply by involving their functional units of our organization	1	2	3	4	5	6	7
32	In my organization there is a clear and consistent set of values in this organization that governs the way we do business	1	2	3	4	5	6	7

(continued)

(continued)

		Strongly agree	*Agree*	*Slightly agree*	*Neither agree or nor disagree*	*Slightly disagree*	*Disagree*	*Strongly disagree*
33	It's compatible for our organization to work in a new and improved ways	1	2	3	4	5	6	7
34	In our organization customers' comments and recommendations often lead the changes of our organization	1	2	3	4	5	6	7
35	In our organization we determine our activity and efforts by coordinating between different units of organization	1	2	3	4	5	6	7
36	In our organization there is a clear strategy for the future	1	2	3	4	5	6	7
37	In our organization, there is widespread agreement about goals of this organization	1	2	3	4	5	6	7
38	We share our thoughts about our organization's future	1	2	3	4	5	6	7

(continued)

(continued)

		Strongly agree	*Agree*	*Slightly agree*	*Neither agree or nor disagree*	*Slightly disagree*	*Disagree*	*Strongly disagree*
39	Our organization motivates a process to create a new private firm-specific knowledge by using formal or informal mechanisms	1	2	3	4	5	6	7
40	Our organization simplifies a process to shift private knowledge to different sectors by using formal or informal mechanism	1	2	3	4	5	6	7
41	Our organization has the strategic activities of people who have an interest in particular institutional arrangement	1	2	3	4	5	6	7
42	Our organization has the strategic activities of people who leverage resource to transform existing institution and create new ones	1	2	3	4	5	6	7

(continued)

(continued)

		Strongly agree	*Agree*	*Slightly agree*	*Neither agree or nor disagree*	*Slightly disagree*	*Disagree*	*Strongly disagree*
43	Our organization has a process to form new public knowledge by the integrated and configured public knowledge which is collected from outside of organization	1	2	3	4	5	6	7
44	Our organization has a process to form new public knowledge by the integrated and configured public knowledge which is collected from inside of organization	1	2	3	4	5	6	7
45	Our organization has a process to increase intellectual capital by strategic activity with open public knowledge	1	2	3	4	5	6	7
46	Our organization uses technology that allows the translation of scientific knowledge into products or process	1	2	3	4	5	6	7

(continued)

(continued)

		Strongly agree	*Agree*	*Slightly agree*	*Neither agree or nor disagree*	*Slightly disagree*	*Disagree*	*Strongly disagree*
47	Our organization uses technology that allows practical application for achievement of my research propose	1	2	3	4	5	6	7
48	Our organization uses technology as a possibility for employee to collaborate with other people of organization	1	2	3	4	5	6	7
49	Our organization uses technology as a possibility for employees to work at one time from different places or learn from one source as a team	1	2	3	4	5	6	7
50	Our organization uses technology as a possibility for employees to work at different places at different time or from different sources as a one team	1	2	3	4	5	6	7

(continued)

(continued)

		Strongly agree	*Agree*	*Slightly agree*	*Neither agree or nor disagree*	*Slightly disagree*	*Disagree*	*Strongly disagree*
51	Our organization uses technologies as a possibility to give chance to illustrate the location (i.e. an individual, specific system or database) of specific types of knowledge	1	2	3	4	5	6	7
52	Our organization uses technology as a possibility to share knowledge, information and experiences which are gained by my experience with individuals	1	2	3	4	5	6	7
53	Our organization uses technology as a possibility to collaborate with other employees by sharing information and knowledge	1	2	3	4	5	6	7
54	Our organization has an opportunity to attend any course and training programs	1	2	3	4	5	6	7
55	Our organization supports changes and desires to learn at work	1	2	3	4	5	6	7

(continued)

(continued)

		Strongly agree	*Agree*	*Slightly agree*	*Neither agree or nor disagree*	*Slightly disagree*	*Disagree*	*Strongly disagree*
56	Our organization employees say "work is important at any given time of my life"	1	2	3	4	5	6	7
57	Our organization has a process to support involvement of employees when there is a decision of work made	1	2	3	4	5	6	7
58	Our organization's employees are encouraged to take responsibility	1	2	3	4	5	6	7
59	Our organization's employees are encouraged to work independently and to control their work themselves	1	2	3	4	5	6	7
60	Our organization has a communication process which is associated to working aim and goals	1	2	3	4	5	6	7

(continued)

(continued)

		Strongly agree	*Agree*	*Slightly agree*	*Neither agree or nor disagree*	*Slightly disagree*	*Disagree*	*Strongly disagree*
61	Our organization has a regular information process which is associated with development's aim and meetings, seminars	1	2	3	4	5	6	7

1. My sex is
   a. male
   b. female
2. My organization belongs to
   a. Social sciences
   b. Engineering sciences
   c. Geology and Geography science
   d. Biology and Agriculture sciences
   e. Physic Mathematics and Chemistry sciences
   f. Academy of Medical science
3. The number of employees in my organization
   a. less than 30
   b. 30–59
   c. 60–79
   d. 80 and more
4. My job is at
   a. chief scientist
   b. senior scientist
   c. mid-level scientist
   d. trainee scientist

e. technical staff and
f. others

5. Length of time I have been working with my present organization

a. 0–2 year
b. 2–5 years
c. 5–8 years
d. Over 8 years

6. Education level attained

a. college certificate
b. bachelor's degree
c. master's degree
d. graduate's degree (doctor degree)
e. post doctor's degree
f. other_______________

7. ______________________If you would like to know the result of this study, please provide your e-mail address here. A summary of results will be emailed to you when the study is completed.

References

Aghion, P., & Howitt, P. (1992). A model of growth through creative destruction. *Econometrica, 60*(2), 323–351. https://doi.org/10.2307/2951599

Aiken, L. S., & West, S. G. (1991). *Multiple regression: Testing and interpreting interactions*. Sage.

Alavi, M., Kayworth, T. M., & Leidner, D. E. (2005). An empirical examination of the influence of organizational culture on knowledge management practices. *Journal of Management Information Systems, 22*(3), 191–224. https://doi.org/10.2753/MIS0742-1222220307

Alavi, M., & Leidner, D. E. (2001). Review: Knowledge management and knowledge management systems: Conceptual foundations and research issues. *MIS Quarterly, 25*(1), 107–136. https://doi.org/10.2307/3250961

Alavi, M., & Robert H. (1999). Knowledge management systems: Issues, challenge, and benefits. *Communications of AIS, 1*(7). http://www.belkcollege.uncc.edu/jpfoley/Readings/artic07.pdf. https://doi.org/10.17705/1CAIS.00107

Al-Hawamdeh, S. (2003). *Knowledge management, cultivating knowledge professionals*. Chandos Publishing. https://doi.org/10.1533/9781780631936

Andrew, C. I., & Dinur, A. (1998). Knowledge management processes and international joint ventures. *Organization Science, 9*(4), 454–468. https://doi.org/10.1287/orsc.9.4.454

Andrews, K. R. (1971). *The concept of corporate strategy*. Dow Jones-Irwin.

Andrews, K. R. (1998). The concept of corporate strategy. In H. Mintzberg, J. B. Quinn & S. Ghoshal, *The strategy process: Revised European edition* (pp. 51–59). Prentice Hall.

B. Dorjgotov, *Enhancing Organizational Effectiveness Through Knowledge Management and Transformational Leadership*, https://doi.org/10.1007/978-981-97-8039-6

Ansoff, H. I. (1965). *Corporate strategy: An analytic approach to business policy for growth and expansion*. McGraw-Hill.

Arthur, J. B. (1994). Effects of human resource systems on manufacturing performance and turnover. *Academy of Management Journal, 37*(3), 670–687. https://doi.org/10.2307/256705

Avolio, B. J., Bass, B. M., & Jung, D. I. (1995). *MLQ multifactor leadership questionnaire: Technical report*. Mindgarden.

Avolio, B. J., Bass, B. M., & Jung, D. I. (1999). Re-examining the components of transformational and transactional leadership using the multifactor leadership questionnaire. *Journal of Occupational and Organizational Psychology, 72*(4), 441–463. https://doi.org/10.1348/096317999166789

Bahra, N. S. (2001). *Competitive knowledge management*. Creative Print & Design. https://doi.org/10.1057/9780230554610

Barney, J. B. (1991). Firms resources and sustained competitive advantage. *Journal of Management, 17*, 99–120. https://doi.org/10.1177/014920639101700108

Barney, J. B., & Zajac, E. J. (1994). Competitive organizational behavior: Towards as organizationally-based theory of competitive advantage. *Strategic Management Journal, 15*, 5–9. https://doi.org/10.1002/smj.4250150902

Baron, R. M., & Kenny, D. A. (1986). The moderator mediator variable distinction in social psychological research: Conceptual, strategic, and statistic considerations. *Journal of Personality and Social Psychology, 51*, 1173–1182. https://doi.org/10.1037/0022-3514.51.6.1173

Bass, B. M. (1985). Leadership: Good, better, best. *Organizational Dynamics, 13*(3), 26–40. https://doi.org/10.1016/0090-2616(85)90028-2

Bass, B. M. (1990). From transactional to transformational leadership: Learning to share the vision. *Organizational Dynamics, 18*(3), 19–31. https://doi.org/10.1016/0090-2616(90)90061-S

Bass, B. M., & Avolio, B. J. (1990a). *Transformational leadership development: Manual for the multifactor leadership questionnaire*. Consulting Psychologist Press.

Bass, B. M., & Avolio, B. J. (1990b). Developing transformational leadership: 1992 and beyond. *Journal of European Industrial Training, 14*(5), 21–27. https://doi.org/10.1108/03090599010135122

Bass, B. M., & Avolio, B. J. (1994). *Improving organizational effectiveness through transformational leadership*. Sage.

Bass, B. M., & Avolio, B. J. (1995). *MLQ multifactor leadership questionnaire*. Second Edition, Sampler Set: Technical Report, Leader Form, Rater Form, and Scoring Key for MLQ Form, x-Short.

Baum, J. R., Locke, E. A., & Kirkpatrick, S. A. (1998). A longitudinal study of vision and vision communication to venture growth in entrepreneurial firms. *Journal of Applied Psychology, 83*, 43–54. https://doi.org/10.1037/0021-9010.83.1.43

Baumol, W. J., & Blinder, A. S. (1994). *Microeconomics: Principles and policy* (6th ed.). Dryden.

Bedeian, A. G., & Zammuto, R. F (1991). *Organizations: Theory and design*. The Dryden Press.

Berson, Y., & Linton, J. D. (2005). An examination of the relationships between leadership style, quality, and employee satisfaction in R&D versus administrative environments. *R&D Management, 35*(1), 51–60. https://doi.org/10.1111/j.1467-9310.2005.00371.x

Bhatt, G. D., & Grover, V. (2005). Types of information technology capabilities and their role in competitive advantage: An empirical study. *Journal of Management Information Systems, 22*(2), 253–277. https://doi.org/10.1080/07421222.2005.11045844

Blackman, A. D., & Lee-Kelley, L. (2006). The role of human resource development in preventing organizational stagnation. *Management Decision, 44*(5), 628–643. https://doi.org/10.1108/00251740610668888

Brad, G., & Max, U. M. (2006). Expanding the HRD role: Improving employee wellbeing and organizational performance. *Human Resource Development International, 9*(4), 563–571. https://doi.org/10.1080/13678860601032684

Brockman, B. K., & Morgan, R. M. (2003). The role of existing knowledge in new product innovativeness and performance. *Decision Sciences, 34*(2), 385–419. https://doi.org/10.1111/1540-5915.02326

Brown, A. D. (1994a). Transformational leadership in tackling technical change. *Journal of General Management, 19*(4), 1–12. https://doi.org/10.1177/030630709401900401

Brown, M. G. (1994b). Is your measurement system well balanced? *Journal for Quality and Participation, 11*(2), 28–32.

Burns, J. M. (1978). *Leadership*. Harper and Row.

Cameron, K. S. (1980). Critical questions in assessing organization effectiveness. *Organizational Dynamics, 9*, 66–80. https://doi.org/10.1016/0090-2616(80)90041-8

Cameron, K. S., & David, A. W. (1983). *Organizational effectiveness: A comparison of multiple models*. Academic Press.

Campbell, J. P. (1987). On the nature of organizational effectiveness. In: P. S. Goodman & J. M. Pennings (Eds.), *New perspectives on organizational effectiveness*. Jossey-Bass.

Carrillo, P., Robinson, H. L., Al-Ghassani, A., & Anumba, C. (2004). Knowledge management in UK constructions: Strategies, resources, and barriers. *Project Management Journal, 35*(1), 46–56. https://doi.org/10.1177/875697280403500105

Choo, C. W. (1996). The knowing organization: How organizations use information to construct meaning, create knowledge and make decisions. *International Journal of Information Management, 16*(5), 329–340. https://doi.org/10.1016/0268-4012(96)00020-5

Clarke, T. E. (2001). *Unique features of an R&D work environment and research scientist and engineers*. Originally Prepared for Rewards, Recognition & Incentives Work Group National Research Council, Canada. http://www.stargate-consultants.ca

Collins, D. J., & Mongomery, C. A. (1995). Competing on resources: Strategy in the 1990s. *Harvard Business Review, 73*(4), 118–128.

Conger, J. A., & Kanungo, R. N. (1987). Toward a behavioral theory of charismatic leadership in organizational settings. *The Academy of Management Review, 12*(4), 637–647. https://doi.org/10.2307/258069

Crawford, C. B. (2005). Effects of transformational leadership and organizational position on knowledge management. *Journal of Knowledge Management, 9*(6), 6–16. https://doi.org/10.1108/13673270510629927

Crawford, C. B., Gould, L. V., & Scott, R. F. (2003). Transformational leader as champion and techie: Implications for leadership educators. *Journal of Leadership Education, 2*(1), 57–73. https://doi.org/10.12806/V2/I1/TF1

Crawford, C. B., & Strohkirch, C. S. (2000). Organizational innovation: Understanding of agents of technological influence. *Electronic Journal of Communication, 10*(1).

Crawford, C. B., & Strohkirch, C. S. (2002). Leadership education and management of knowledge organizations: An overview. *Journal of Leadership Education, 1*(2), 18–33. https://doi.org/10.12806/V1/I2/RF2

Custer, R. L. (1995). Examining the dimensions of technology. *International Journal of Technology and Design Education, 5*, 219–244. https://doi.org/10.1007/BF00769905

Daft, R. L. (1988). *Organization theory and design*. West Publishing Co.

Davenport, T. H., & Prusak, L. (1998). *Working knowledge: How organizations manage what they know*. Harvard Business School Press.

Deluga, R. J. (1990). The effects of transformational, transactional, and laissez faire leadership characteristics on subordinate influencing behavior. *Basic & Applied Social Psychology, 11*(2), 191–203. https://doi.org/10.1207/s15324834basp1102_6

Denison, D. R. (1990). *Corporate culture and organizational effectiveness*. Wiley.

Denison, D. R., & Mishra, A. K. (1995). Toward a theory of organizational culture and effectiveness. *Organization Science, 6*(2), 204–223. https://doi.org/10.1287/orsc.6.2.204

Denison, D. R., Stephanie, H., & Paulo, G. (2003). Corporate culture and organizational effectiveness: Is Asia different from the rest of the world?

Organizational Dynamics, 33(1), 98–109. https://doi.org/10.1016/j.orgdyn.2003.11.008

Dess, G. G., & Davis, P. S. (1984). Porter's generic strategies as determinants of strategic group membership and organization performance. *Academic Management Journal, 27*(3), 467–488. https://doi.org/10.5465/256040

Dorf, R. C. (2001). *Technology, humans, and society: Toward a sustainable world* (pp. 65–82). Academic Press: 92101-4495.

Drongelen, I. C. K.-V., de Weerd-Nederhof, P. C., & Olaf, A. M. F. (1996). Describing the issues of knowledge management in R&D: Towards a communication and analysis tool. *R&D Management, 26*(3), 213–230. https://doi.org/10.1111/j.1467-9310.1996.tb00957.x

Elkins, T., & Keller, R. T. (2003). Leadership in research and development organizations: A literature review and conceptual framework. *The Leadership Quarterly, 14*, 587–596. https://doi.org/10.1016/S1048-9843(03)00053-5

Etzioni, A. (1964). *Modern organization—Foundations of modern sociology*. Prentice-Hall Inc.

Ezra, O. O., & Janet, G. S. (2009). The role of knowledge management in enhancing government service-delivery in Kenya. *SA Jnl Libs & Information Science, 75*(1), 28–39.

Fey, C. F., & Denison, D. R. (2003). Organizational culture and effectiveness: Can American theory be applied in Russia? *Organization Science, 14*(6), 686–706. https://doi.org/10.1287/orsc.14.6.686.24868

Forbes, D. (1998). Measuring the unmeasurable: Empirical studies of nonprofit organization effectiveness from 1977 to 1997. *Nonprofit & Voluntary Sector Quarterly, 27*, 183–202. https://doi.org/10.1177/0899764098272005

Ganbat, B. (2003). *Research and development policy in Mongolia: Current situation and suggestions for future* (Master's thesis). IDES of Hiroshima University, Higashi Hiroshima, Japan.

Ganzorig, Ch. (2009). *Knowledge colonization*. Unpublished paper, National University of Mongolia, Ulaanbaatar, Mongolia.

Gefen, D., Straub, D., & Boudreau, M.C. (2000). Structural equation modeling and regression: Guidelines for research practice. *Communications of AIS, 4*(7), 1–80. https://doi.org/10.17705/1CAIS.00407

Godin, B., & Doré, C. (2006). *Measuring the impacts of science: Beyond the economic dimension*. Working paper, mimeo.

Gold, A. H., Malhotra, A., & Segars, A. H. (2001). Knowledge management: An organizational capabilities perspective. *Journal of Management Information Systems, 18*(1), 185–214. https://doi.org/10.1080/07421222.2001.11045669

Gretchen, B. J., Streit, L. D., & Binkley, J. S. (2003). Assessing and improving the effectiveness of national research laboratories. *IEEE Transactions on*

Engineering Management, 50(2), 228–235. https://doi.org/10.1109/TEM.2003.810820

Griffith, R. (2000). *How important is business R&D for economic growth and should the government subsides it?* Published by the Institute for Fiscal Studies. https://doi.org/10.1920/bn.ifs.2000.0012. http://www.ifs.org.uk/publications/1720

Griffith, R., Redding, S., & Van Reenen, J. (2000). *Mapping the two faces of R&D: Productivity growth in a panel of OECD industries* (Discussion Paper no. 2457). Centre for Economic Policy Research. https://doi.org/10.2139/ssrn.229400

Guillermo, R.-O. (2003). *A knowledge management and quality model for R&D organizations* (V. Palade, R. J. Howlett, & L. C. Jain, Eds.: KES 2003, LNAI 2773, pp. 1000–1007). Springer-Verlag.

Hause, O. R. (2000). *Relationships between organizational culture strength and organizational effectiveness in an electrical utility company* (Dissertation work). University of Georgia, Athens, GA.

Hax, A. C., & Majluf, N. S. (1996). *The strategy concept and process: A pragmatic approach*. Prentice-Hall. http://www.des.calstate.edu/glossary.html

Herman, R. D., & Renz, D. O. (2004). Doing things right: Effectiveness in local nonprofit organizations, a panel study. *Public Administration Review, 64*(6), 694–703. https://doi.org/10.1111/j.1540-6210.2004.00416.x

Herman, R. D., & Renz, D. O. (2008). Advancing nonprofit organizational effectiveness research and theory, nine theses. *Nonprofit Management & Leadership, 18*(4), 399–415. https://doi.org/10.1002/nml.195

House, R. J., & Baetz, M. L. (1979). Leadership: Some empirical generalizations and new research directions. In B. M. Staw (Ed.), *Research in organizational behavior* (Vol. 1, pp. 399–401). Elsevier.

Howell, J. M., & Higgins, C. A. (1990). Champions of technological innovation. *Administrative Science Quarterly, 35*, 317–341. https://doi.org/10.2307/2393393

Huber, G. P. (1991). Organizational learning: The contributing processes and the literatures. *Organization Science, 2*(1), 88–115. https://doi.org/10.1287/orsc.2.1.88

Huselid, M. A. (1995). The impact on human resource management practices on turnover, productivity, and corporate financial performance. *Academy of Management Journal, 38*(3), 635–672. https://doi.org/10.2307/256741

Huselid, M. A., Jackson, S. E., & Schuler, R. S. (1997). Technical and strategic human resource management effectiveness as determinants of firm performance. *Academy of Management Journal, 40*(1), 171–188. https://doi.org/10.2307/257025

Ichijo, K. (2002). Knowledge exploitation and knowledge exploration: Two strategies for knowledge creating companies. In *The strategic management of intellectual capital and organizational knowledge* (pp. 477–483). Oxford University Press. https://doi.org/10.1093/oso/9780195138665.003.0026

Irma, B. F., & Rajiv, S. (2001). Organizational knowledge management: A contingency perspective. *Journal of Management Information Systems, 18*(1), 23–55. https://doi.org/10.1080/07421222.2001.11045676

Janz, B. D., & Prasarnphanich, P. (2003). Understanding the antecedents of effective knowledge management: The importance of a knowledge-centered culture. *Decision Sciences, 34*(2), 351–384. https://doi.org/10.1111/1540-5915.02328

Jain, R. K., & Triandis, H. C. (1997) *Management of research and development organizations: Managing the unmanageable* (2nd ed.). Wiley.

Johns, H. E., & Moser, H. R. (1989). From trait to transformation: The evolution of leadership theories. *Education, 110*(1), 115–122.

Keesing, R. M. (1974). Theories of culture. *Annual Review of Anthropology, 3*, 73–79. https://doi.org/10.1146/annurev.an.03.100174.000445

Keller, R. T. (1992). Transformational leadership and performance of research and development project groups. *Journal of Management, 18*, 489–501. https://doi.org/10.1177/014920639201800304

Kermally, S. (2002). *Effective knowledge management: A best practice blueprint*. Wiley.

Kim, S., & Lee, H. (2006). The impact of organizational context and information technology on employee knowledge-sharing capabilities. *Public Administration Review, 66*(3), 370–385. https://doi.org/10.1111/j.1540-6210.2006.00595.x

Klenke, K. (1994). Information technologies as drivers of emergent organizational forms: A leadership perspective. In S. Smiths, R. Baskerville, O. Ngwenyama, & J. de Gross (Eds.), *Transforming organizations with information technology*. Proceeding of the IFIP WG 8.2 Conference (pp. 323–334). Amsterdam.

Kogut, B., & Zander, U. (1992). Knowledge of the firm, combinative capabilities, and the replication of technology. *Organization Science, 3*, 383–397. https://doi.org/10.1287/orsc.3.3.383

Koh, W. T. H. (2006). Singapore's transition to innovation-based economic growth: Infrastructure, institutions and Government's role. *R&D Management, 36*(2), 143–160. https://doi.org/10.1111/j.1467-9310.2006.00422.x

Kondra, A. Z., & Hurst, D. C. (2009). Institutional processes of organizational culture. *Culture and Organization, 15*(1), 39–58. https://doi.org/10.1080/14759550802709541

Krull, J. L., & Mackinnon, D. P. (1999). Multilevel mediation modeling in group based intervention studies. *Evaluation Review, 23*, 418–444. https://doi.org/10.1177/0193841X9902300404

Krull, J. L., & Mackinnon, D. P. (2001). Multilevel modeling of individual and group level mediated effects. *Multivariate Behavioral Research, 36*, 249–277. https://doi.org/10.1207/S15327906MBR3602_06

Kucza, T. (2001). *Knowledge management process model*. Espoo 2001. Technical Research Centre of Finland, VTT Publications. http://www.mendeley.com/research/

Lado, A. A., & Wilson, M. C. (1994). Human resource systems and sustained competitive advantage: A competency-based perspective. *Academy of Management Review, 19*(4), 699–727. https://doi.org/10.2307/258742

Lawler, E. E. (2005). From human resource management to organizational effectiveness. *Human Resource Management, 44*(2), 165–169. https://doi.org/10.1002/hrm.20059

Lee, H., Chae, Y., & Suh, Y. (2004). Knowledge conversion with information technology of Korean companies. *Total Quality Management, 15*(3), 279–294. https://doi.org/10.1080/1478336042000183433

Lee, H., & Choi, B. (2000). *Knowledge management enablers, processes, and organizational performance: An integration and empirical examination*. APDSI 2000 Full Paper.

Lee, H., & Choi, B. (2003). Knowledge management enablers, processes, and organizational performance: An integrative view and empirical examination. *Journal of Management Information Systems, 20*(1), 179–228. https://doi.org/10.1080/07421222.2003.11045756

Lee, H., & Suh, Y. (2003). Knowledge conversion with information technology of Korean companies. *Business Process Management Journals, 9*(3), 317–336. https://doi.org/10.1108/14637150310477911

Lee, L. T., & Sukoco, B. M. (2007). The effects of entrepreneurial orientation and knowledge management capability on organizational effectiveness in Taiwan: The moderating role of social capital. *International Journal of Management, 24*(3), 549–572.

Leonard, D., & Sensiper, S. (1998). The role of tacit knowledge in group innovation. *California Management Review, 40*(3), 112–132. https://doi.org/10.2307/41165946

Lepak, D. P., & Snell, S. A. (1999). The human resource architecture: Toward a theory of human capital allocation and development. *Academy of Management Review, 24*, 31–48. https://doi.org/10.2307/259035

Liao, S. (2003). Review: Knowledge management technologies and applications-literature review from 1995 to 2002. *Expert Systems with Applications, 25*, 155–164. https://doi.org/10.1016/S0957-4174(03)00043-5

Locke, E. A., & Latham, G. P. (1990). *A theory of goal setting and task performance*. Prentice-Hall.

Lusthaus, C., Adrien, M.-h., Anderson, G., & Montalvan, G. P. (2002). *Organizational assessment: A framework for improving performance*. International Development Research Center.

Mahoney, T. A., & Weitzel, W. (1969). Managerial models of organizational effectiveness. *Administrative Science Quarterly, 14*(3), 357–365. https://doi.org/10.2307/2391131

March, J. G. (1991). Exploration and exploitation in organisational learning. *Organization Science, 2*, 71–87. https://doi.org/10.1287/orsc.2.1.71

March, J. G., & Sutton, R. I. (1997). Organizational performance as a dependent variable. *Organizational Science, 8*(6), 698–706. https://doi.org/10.1287/orsc.8.6.698

Marlene, A. D. (2002). *The relationship between human resource management and organizational effectiveness in non-profit organizations*. Dissertation work, the Ohio State University.

Matsumoto, M., Yokota, S., Naito, K., & Itoh, J. (2009). Development of a model to estimate the economic impacts of R&D output of public research institutes. *R&D Management, 40*(1), 91–100. https://doi.org/10.1111/j.1467-9310.2009.00578.x

Matusik, S. F., & Hill, C. W. L. (1998). The utilization of contingent work, knowledge creation, and competitive advantage. *The Academy of Management Review, 23*(4), 680–697. https://doi.org/10.2307/259057

McDermott, R., & O'Dell, C. (2001). Overcoming cultural barriers to sharing knowledge. *Journal of Knowledge Management, 5*(1), 76–85. https://doi.org/10.1108/13673270110384428

McGuire, S., Hardy, C., & Lawrence, T. B. (2004). Institutional entrepreneurship in emerging fields: HIV/AIDS treatment advocacy in Canada. *Academy of Management Journal, 46*(5), 657–679. https://doi.org/10.2307/20159610

Meyers, P. W., & Wilemon, D. (1989). Learning in new technology development teams. *Journal of Product and Innovation in Management, 6*, 79–88. https://doi.org/10.1111/1540-5885.620079

Miles, R., & Snow, C. (1978). *Organizational strategy, structure, and process*. McGraw-Hill. https://doi.org/10.2307/257544

Mitcham, C. (1979). Philosophy and the history of technology. In G. Bugliarello (Ed.), *The history and philosophy of technology* (pp. 163–201). University of Illinois Press.

Nahapiet, J., & Ghoshal, S. (1998). Social capital, intellectual capital, and the organizational advantage. *Academy of Management Review, 23*(2), 242–266. https://doi.org/10.2307/259373

NSTF (National Science and Technology Foundation). (2002). *Annual report, Ulaanbaatar, Mongolia*.

Nonaka, I. (1991). The knowledge-creating company. *Harvard Business Review, 69*, 96–104.

Nonaka, I. (1994). A dynamic theory of organizational knowledge creation. *Organizational Science, 5*(1), 14–37. https://doi.org/10.1287/orsc.5.1.14

Nonaka, I., & Konno, N. (1998). The concept of "Ba" building a foundation of knowledge creation. *California Management Review, 40*(3), 40–54. https://doi.org/10.2307/41165942

Nonaka, I., & Takeuchi, H. (1995). *The knowledge-creating company*. Oxford University Press. https://doi.org/10.1093/oso/9780195092691.001.0001

Nonaka, I., Toyama, R., & Konno, N. (2000). SECI, Ba and leadership: A unified model of dynamic knowledge creation. *Long Range Planning, 33*, 5–34. https://doi.org/10.1016/S0024-6301(99)00115-6

OECD (Organization for Economic Cooperation and Development). (1993). *The annual report of the OECD: The measurement of scientific and technological activities*. OECD.

Ott, J. S. (1989). *The organizational culture perspective*. Malloy Lithographing Inc.

O'Reilly, C. (1989). Corporations, culture, and commitment: Motivation and social control in organizations. *California Management Review, 18*, 9–25. https://doi.org/10.2307/41166580

Porter, M. E. (1985). *Competitive advantage creating and sustaining superior performance*. Free Press.

Price, J. L. (1972). The study of organizational effectiveness. *Sociological Quarterly, 13*, 3–15. https://doi.org/10.1111/j.1533-8525.1972.tb02100.x

Quinn, J. B. (1980). Strategy for change. In H. Mintzberg & J. B. Quinn, *Readings in the strategy process* (3rd ed., pp. 3–10). Prentice-Hall, 1998.

Ramanathan, K. (2008). *Evolution of research and development (R&D) management*. ppt., Valorization of Research and Development. Joint CSIR/HRDC and UNESCAP-APCTT Program for the Mongolian Science and Technology, UB, Mongolia.

Rastogi, P. N. (2000). Knowledge management and intellectual capital—The new virtuous reality of competitiveness. *Human System Management, 19*(1), 39–49. https://doi.org/10.3233/HSM-2000-19105

Rauch, A., Frese, M., & Utsch, A. (2005). Effects of human capital and long-term human resources development and utilization on employment growth of small-scale businesses: A causal analysis. *Entrepreneurship Theory and Practice, 29*, 681–698.

Reichers, A. E., & Schneider, B. (1990). Climate and culture: An evolution of constructs. In B. Schneider (Ed.), *Organizational climate and culture* (pp. 5–39). Josey-Bass Inc.

Sanchez, R. (2001). *Managing knowledge into competence: The five learning cycles of the competent organization*. British Library Cataloguing in Publication data, Oxford University Press Inc.

Science and Technology (S&T) Plan of Mongolia, 2007–2020. (2007). Ministry of Education, Culture and Science, Ulaanbaatar, Mongolia.

Schein, E. H. (1981). Does Japanese management style have a message for American managers? *Sloan Management Review, 23*, 55–68.

Schein, E. H. (1984). Coming to a new awareness of organizational culture. *Sloan Management Review, 25*, 3–16.

Schein, E. H. (1985). *Organizational culture and leadership: A dynamic view*. Jossey-Bass.

Schein, E. H. (1988). *Organizational culture* (Working paper). Sloan School of Management.

Schein, E. H. (1990). Organizational culture. *American Psychologist, 45*(2), 109–119. https://doi.org/10.1037/0003-066X.45.2.109

Schultze, U., & Leidner, D. (2002). Studying knowledge management in information systems research: Discourses and theoretical assumptions. *MIS Quarterly, 26*(3), 213–242. https://doi.org/10.2307/4132331

Scott, W. R. (1977). Effectiveness in organizational effectiveness studies. In P. S. Goodman & J. M. Pennings (Eds.) *New perspectives on organizational effectiveness* (1st ed.). Jossey-Bass.

Sharabi, M., & Harpaz, I. (2010). Improving employees' work centrality improves organizational performance: Work events and work centrality relationships. *Human Resource Development International, 13*(4), 379–392. https://doi.org/10.1080/13678868.2010.501960

Shera, P. J., & Lee, V. C. (2004). Information technology as a facilitator for enhancing dynamic capabilities through knowledge management. *Information & Management, 41*, 933–945. https://doi.org/10.1016/j.im.2003.06.004

Short, J. C., Palmer, T. P., & Ketchen, D. J., Jr. (2003). Multi-level influences on firm performance: Insights from the resource-based view and strategic groups research. *Multi-level Issues in Organizational Behavior and Strategy Research in Multi-Level Issues, 2*, 155–187. https://doi.org/10.1016/S1475-9144(03)02010-1

Smith, T. A. (2006). *Knowledge management and its capabilities linked to the business strategy for organizational effectiveness* (Doctoral dissertation). Available from Dissertation and Thesis database (UMI No. 3250678).

Snow, C. C., & Hambrick, D. C. (1980). Measuring organizational strategies: Some theoretical and methodological problems. *Academy of Management Review, 5*(4), 527–538. https://doi.org/10.2307/257458

Sosik, J. J., Kahai, S. S., & Avolio, B. J. (2003). Transformational leadership, conservation and creativity: Evidence from Korea. *Academy of Management Journal, 46*(6), 703–714. https://doi.org/10.2307/30040662

Sparkes, J. R., & Miyake, M. (2000). Knowledge transfer and human resource development practices: Japanese firms in Brazil and Mexico. *International Business Review, 9*, 599–612. https://doi.org/10.1016/S0969-5931(00)00021-4

Speed, J. (1989). Oh Mr. Porter! A re-appraisal of competitive strategy. *Marketing Intelligence and Planning, 7*(5/6), 8–11. https://doi.org/10.1108/EUM0000000001043

Steers, R. (1975). Problems in the measurement of organizational effectiveness. *Administrative Science Quarterly, 20*, 546–548. https://doi.org/10.2307/2392022

Takeuchi, H., & Nonaka, I. (1986, January–February). The new product development game. *Harvard Business Review*.

Turban, E., & Aronson, J. E. (2001). *Decision support systems and intelligent systems* (6th ed.). Prentice Hall.

van der Spek, R., & Spijkervet, A. (1997). *Knowledge management: Dealing intelligently with knowledge*. Knowledge Management Network, Kenniscentrum CIBIT and CSC, ISBN 90-75709-02-1.

Van Seters, D. A., & Field, R. H. G. (1989). The evolution of leadership theory. *Journal of OCM, 3*(3), 29–45. https://doi.org/10.1108/09534819010142139

Vecchio, R. P. (1995). *Organizational behavior*. Harcourt Brace and Co.

World Bank. (1998). *World Development Report 1998/1999: Knowledge for development*. World Bank. https://doi.org/10.1596/978-0-1952-1118-4

Yamin, S., Mavond, F., Gunasekaran, A. B., & Sarros, J. C. (1997). A study of competitive strategy, organisational innovation and organisational performance among Australian manufacturing companies. *International Journal of Production Economics, 52*, 161–172. https://doi.org/10.1016/S0925-5273(96)00104-1

Yang, C. W., Fang, S. C., & Lin, J. L. (2009). Organisational knowledge creation strategies: A conceptual framework. *International Journal of Information Management, 30*, 231–238. https://doi.org/10.1016/j.ijinfomgt.2009.08.005

Yang, J.-t, & Wan, C.-s. (2003). Advancing organizational effectiveness and knowledge management implementation. *Journal of Tourist Management, 25*, 593–601. https://doi.org/10.1016/j.tourman.2003.08.002

Young, G., Sapienza, H., & Baumer, D. (1999). The influence of flexibility in buyer-seller relationships on the productivity of knowledge. *Journal of Business Reviews, 56*(6), 443–451. https://doi.org/10.1016/S0148-2963(01)00243-0

Yukl, G. (1989). Managerial leadership: A review of theory and research. *Journal of Management, 15*(2), 251–289. https://doi.org/10.1177/014920638901500207

Yukl, G. (1999). An evaluate essay on current conceptions of effective leadership. *European Journal of Work and Organizational Psychology, 8*(1), 33–48. https://doi.org/10.1080/135943299398429

Yukl, G. (2008). How leaders influence organizational effectiveness. *The Leadership Quarterly, 19*, 708–722. https://doi.org/10.1016/j.leaqua.2008.09.008

Yukl, G., & Van Fleet, D. D. (1992). Theory and research on leadership in organizations. In M. D. Dunnette & L. M. Hough (Eds.), *Handbook of industrial and organizational psychology* (Vol. 3, 2nd ed., pp. 147–197). Consulting Psychologists.

Zammuto, R. F. (1982). *Assessing organizational effectiveness*. State University of New York Press.

Zheng, W., Yang, B., & McLean, G. N. (2009). Linking organizational culture, structure, strategy, and organizational effectiveness: Mediating role of knowledge management. *Journal of Business Research, 63*(7), 763–771. https://doi.org/10.1016/j.jbusres.2009.06.005

Index

B. Dorjgotov, *Enhancing Organizational Effectiveness Through Knowledge Management and Transformational Leadership*, https://doi.org/10.1007/978-981-97-8039-6

SPRINGER NATURE

GPSR Compliance

The European Union's (EU) General Product Safety Regulation (GPSR) is a set of rules that requires consumer products to be safe and our obligations to ensure this.

If you have any concerns about our products, you can contact us on ProductSafety@springernature.com

In case Publisher is established outside the EU, the EU authorized representative is:

Springer Nature Customer Service Center GmbH
Europaplatz 3
69115 Heidelberg, Germany

The manufacturer's authorised representative in the EU is Springer Nature Customer Service Centre GmbH, Europaplatz 3, 69115 Heidelberg, Germany. If you have any concerns regarding our products, please contact ProductSafety@springernature.com

Printed and bound by CPI Group (UK) Ltd, Croydon, CR0 4YY

01/10/2026

02225978-0009